THE FRAGILE CURTAIN

D1430744

KAREN BURTON MAINS

David C. Cook Publishing Co.
ELGIN. ILLINOIS—WESTON. ONTARIO

Grateful acknowledgment is made to the following publishers for permission to reprint copyrighted material:

Excerpt by LaVonne Platt in *More-with-Less Cookbook* by Doris Janzen Longacre, copyright 1976, Herald Press, Scottdale, Pa.

"The Edge of Hell," by Lynnell Mickelsen. Reprinted from *Campus Life* Magazine, May 1980. Published by Youth for Christ International, Wheaton, Ill.

"Great Is Thy Faithfulness," by Thomas O. Chisholm, lyrics reprinted by special permission of Hope Publishing, Carol Stream, Ill.

"Dirge Without Music," by Edna St. Vincent Millay, from *Collected Poems,* Harper and Row, © 1928, 1955 by Edna St. Vincent Millay and Norma Millay Ellis.

A portion of the royalties from this book is being donated to Food for the Hungry International, Scottsdale, Ariz.

THE FRAGILE CURTAIN
© 1981 Karen Burton Mains

Published by David C. Cook Publishing Co., Elgin, IL 60120
Book design by The Cioni Artworks

First paperback printing: September 1983

Photographic credits:
Page 14, David Singer
      46, Marty Hardison
      64, Mickey Moore

Special thanks to Food for the Hungry for their photographic contributions, particularly Vivian Angerami.
Printed in the United States of America

LC: 81-67802

Library of Congress Cataloging in Publication Data
Mains, Karen Burton.
    The fragile curtain.
    1. Refugees.
HV640.M33   362.8'7   81-67802
ISBN 0-89191-795-0   AACR2

To Larry and Lorraine Ward
and to others like them
who have seen the world in torment thousands of times
and are still moved to tears.

And to us all—
may our private pains make us common.

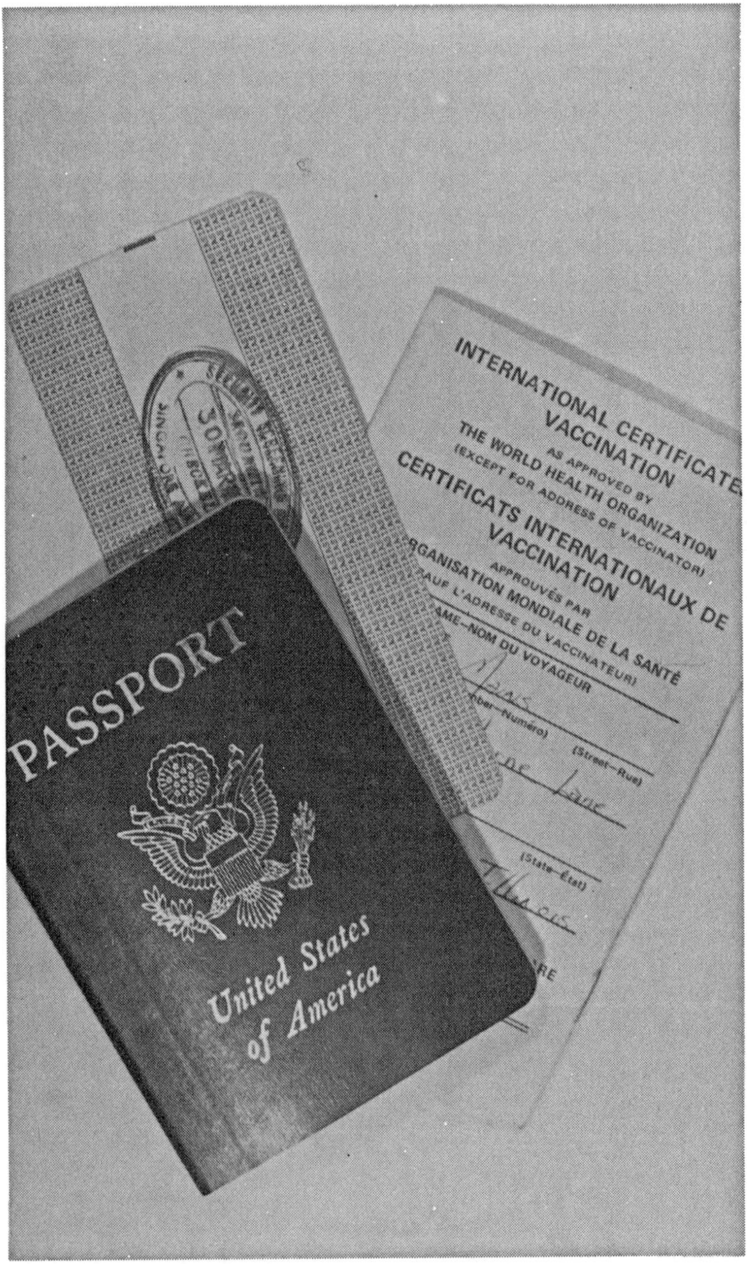
PASSPORT
United States of America
INTERNATIONAL CERTIFICATE
VACCINATION
AS APPROVED BY
THE WORLD HEALTH ORGANIZATION
(EXCEPT FOR ADDRESS OF VACCINATOR)
CERTIFICATS INTERNATIONAUX DE
VACCINATION
APPROUVÉS PAR
ORGANISATION MONDIALE DE LA SANTÉ
(SAUF L'ADRESSE DU VACCINATEUR)
NOM DU VOYAGEUR
(Street—Rue)
(State—État)

I Two Worlds

1   The Fragile Curtain
Chicago, Illinois, April 2, 1981

I have lived all my life behind a fragile curtain. Of delicate substance, it has nevertheless insulated me. It is formed from the fine threads of the small worlds I know: backyard worlds, the familiar ground of home and work, the thoughts of people I cherish.

Illusion is my curtain's name, the illusion that all is well in my world, that I am safe. Neither is it mine alone. Each human lives behind his own illusion. Seeing, we do not see. We are unaware of our myopia.

This sheer hanging is flimsy and easily torn, yet it seems it must always be taken by violence. Despair can part it. Ungentle hands can rend it. Death severs it. Truth can yank it down.

My curtain of illusion was torn when I made a traveling survey of the refugee camps of the world in the spring of 1980. My invitation to go there came from Dr. Larry Ward, the president of an international relief and development organization, Food for the Hungry.

My assignment was to see with fresh eyes, then to tell. Our six-week trip wound from the refugee warehouses in Hong Kong, to Singapore, to the camps in Thailand, across Nepal and India, to Pakistan, then dropped down into Africa, focusing on Kenya and Somalia. It was literally a trip around the world.

I was not prepared for the beauty of the refugee. I went to interpret the pain and suffering of their world, and was overcome when I discovered that the refugee translated for me the meaning of the pain and suffering of my own.

Ever since returning from that spring journey, I have found myself measuring two worlds: the one around me and the one beyond. Amazingly, it is the far one (the world of the camps and the thousands) that best helps me understand the world that is near.

My fragile curtain has been shredded. I can no longer hide behind these frail remnants of security. Loss grins at me. The flexing fingers of hurt—my own and others—has touched me.

It always takes courage to step outside. Birth, beginnings of any kind, are risky. But I want to see. . . .

II   Meeting Places

1 Celebration

Wheaton, Illinois, and the South China Sea, March 9, 1980
Singapore Harbor, Malaysia, March 29, 1980

On March 9, just a few days before I left for Asia, my husband's family celebrated my father-in-law's birthday, one day early. It was a rare event, one of those special times when the curtains that separate us drift apart, affording rare glimpses of each other.

My brother-in-law, a surgeon, relaxed in his chair, leaning back as head of the table in his own house. The small children, invited by celebration, edged closer and perched on the corner of some adult's seat, sharing space until they were drawn within the circle.

The ritual of birthday began, the liturgy was enacted, the song chanted, the dancing flames extinguished. Someone probed gently at a familiar peculiarity of a loved one's personality. Laughter rose like incense, binding our crossed communion.

One of the teens (we seem to have more these days) mentioned a research paper dealing with the latest political candidates. A college student (more of these as well) animatedly defended a point. Evolving opinions were challenged. Then conversation began, real conversation, not old words pacing around frayed topics but new explorations prancing up fresh paths.

It flowed, this saying and telling and thinking aloud. It ebbed between persons and eddied in pools of agreement and broke against disparate opinions. Even the smallest child found room to wade a little, while the rest of us swam into economics and literature and natural science and religion. Again and again laughter came. The muted hues of my sister-in-law's rooms embraced us.

It was a wonderful birthday party, a rare evening, an evening of warming at each other's fires, a family gathering. It was the kind of sharing people long for when they are alone or far away or grieving. It was a moment few ever hold, and then only infrequently.

Halfway across the world a gathering of another kind was taking place. A celebration, which was separated from ours by time and space, but linked to my father-in-law's birthday by the joy, the eternal quality of the moment.

Somewhere in the triangle of high sea between Southeast Asia, the Philippines, and Malaysia, fifty-four Vietnamese boat people were being fished out of the waters. The fishermen were crew members of the *Acuna*, a Second World War fighting ship, now recommissioned for another kind of battle. Its supporting organization is a worldwide Christian aid agency, Food for the Hungry.

Although the engine of the refugees' boat had been disabled and they had floated without food and water for three days, these were fortunate people. They had been unmarauded by pirates. In the previous *Acuna* rescue, an older woman had climbed aboard only to collapse once on deck. Her two young daughters had been raped numerous times before her horrified eyes.

The refugees who had been gathered from the waters that March day in 1980 had been fortunate to slip through a keyhole in the violent seasonal weather. Leaving the night-choked coastline of Vietnam some five days before, they had trailed the monsoon season. Their stealthy March departure had also avoided the typhoons, which rage from July to November, rising pugnacious in the South China Sea and then belching across Indochina and the Philippines.

They had ended their journey with their starting number of passengers. They were a most fortunate fifty-four. Some estimates place the toll of sea deaths for the previous year as high as three hundred thousand Vietnamese.

I am told that *Acuna* means "a meeting place in the waters." If so, it was a propitious meeting for these, who would only know how really fortunate they were when they reached their first place of asylum and began to compare tales with other refugees.

The stories of the atrocities of the pirates who leech life from the vast archipelago that tattoos these waters are enough to convince any skeptic of the innate depravity of man. Though some only rob, exchanging food and water and fuel for their marauding, others murder and plunder and maim. An account, reported in the book, *The Boat People,* is unfortunately all too typical:

> The pirates tied them up and threw them into the water. The remaining people were tied up too and locked in the hold after being stripped of their belongings. After this, the pirates came again to our

boat to pillage and rape people. One person was killed after being dealt a blow with an iron bar. Another had his finger cut off because he was unable to pull off his wedding ring. When everything was looted, the pirates hurried to go. They released the men they kept in the hold, and kicked them back to our boat. Some fell into the water and drowned with their hands bound behind their backs.

I met the fifty-four who had just been rescued by the *Acuna* on March 29, 1980, in Singapore harbor where they had been delayed by the inevitable machinery of immigration red tape. Word had reached my host, Larry Ward, that off-loading, or disembarking, was imminent. If we hurried, we might be present. The next morning found us waiting for a water taxi to speed us alongside the rescue vessel.

There hadn't been time for breakfast, and my stomach is notorious for its misbehavior in small airplanes and boats. I eyed the oil slicks and the old wooden transports blackened by years of plying these waters. Grime and grease and the carbon of diesel smoke were indelibly smeared into their sides. I took one whiff of the pungent harbor odor and felt the familiar nausea churning. Gratefully, I gobbled a croissant my host's wife had wrapped in a paper napkin and stored in her purse.

Having anchored my stomach, we boarded; the boat taxi sped off. After a while the *Acuna* was spotted. We came alongside, plunged up the swaying shipside ladder, were greeted by captain and crew, then looked for those fortunate fifty-four.

I was not prepared for the word becoming flesh. These boat people I had read about, whose political and historical background I had researched, were real: breath and flesh; substance, joint, and sinew; spirit, defiance, and despair; joy and bewilderment.

I had expected symbols, caricatures even, of the hounded and the oppressed. What I discovered instead, were real people who all talked in a buoyant chatter at the same time, whose black eyes and hair repeated in countless duplicate were all the more beautiful because of the repetition. These were people who told jokes in broken English, who slipped gingerly in and out of the traditional split-toe sandal while I fumbled with buckles and straps, and who were unerring in their offers of grace and hospitality.

Illusion can be an inadequate guide.

A tarp had been spread over part of the ship's deck for them to live beneath as they waited for permission to disembark. They gathered in front of it. Then the news was given: off-loading would take place today. Smiles broke; cheers bannered the air; children clapped their hands, bounced. Genial commotion announced itself.

My eye caught a young woman who squirmed when the question was asked if anyone spoke English. "No, no," she protested. "My Engleesh very bad. Speak very leetle."

I was undaunted, however. Whatever "leetle" she spoke was worlds beyond my nonexistent Vietnamese. Besides I had learned that words often convey less than we want them to. The language of the soul, of emotion, had become more important to me since I had arrived in Asia. I was becoming a master at detecting the meaning behind words.

The young woman was twenty-seven years old and had brought with her a sister twenty-five, two younger brothers sixteen and fourteen, then an extended family member, perhaps a cousin or niece around eighteen. She had left her mother, age fifty-six, one sister twenty-two, and a small brother ten.

"My father," she explained. "He is een jail." (She crosses her hands at the wrists.) "He soldier. Officer. Communists jail him. You understand?"

I was beginning to. Enormity opened its sleepy eyes.

She continued, telling me that the captain (that man over there) had made the boat. He was lounging silently, watchfully, against the side of the canopy while his little wife, soft-fleshed and full of shy smiles, gathered their possessions, a few bundles, and their children into order. I counted eight children, one an infant sleeping contentedly in the middle of the confusion.

Without words I understood the captain's grim silence. He was a man who had successfully completed a task. Weather-beaten, his face hardening into set lines and ridges, he had built a boat. His hands had planed the planks—slivers piercing his finger pads, soft shavings curling to the floor. He had fitted the joints, caulked the seams, smoothed the hold. His set-jaw determination had worked seaworthiness—had willed it—into the craft. A new Noah, destiny had closed the door to his existence in his own land. He had sailed out of the deluge, piloting wife and children to freedom.

"Were you not afraid of pirates?" I asked the young woman.

She shook her head. No understanding crossed her eyes. I wrote the words on a piece of paper. FEAR. AFRAID. She shook her head again. Her

English did not include these terrible words.

"Excuse me," she said. "We all fix food. Now, my turn. Excuse me please."

I watched her go, glad for the interruption. I needed a moment to absorb what I had just heard and what I had not heard. Here was a young woman who had left her homeland and said good-bye to a mother she would most likely never see again. She had taken upon herself the responsibility of the lives of younger siblings and had turned her face to chance, to an absolutely unknown future. In order to escape detection (she had been captured once before while attempting to flee) she had brought nothing more than the clothes on her back.

Why? What forces these kinds of choices upon a young woman, one alone with no adult male to protect her, to die for her?

Suddenly, from the ship's galley, she reappeared. "My seester and I. We change. She cook food." The flashing smile shone on me.

Why? Why did you come? That was the question I had to hear answered. What on earth would impel this displacement, these utterly final decisions? Why impose upon oneself severance and wandering and homelessness? Why cut oneself away from the familiar places of memory renewal, like the bamboo stand of slender trees that dropped their yellow leaves on the footpath by her home?

Why abandon language? I thought of Mowbray's poignant lament when hearing King Richard's sentence of banishment upon him:

> "The language I have learnt these forty years,
> My native English, now I must forego;
> And now my tongue's use is to me no more
> Than an unstringed viol or a harp. . . .
> Within my mouth you have enjail'd my tongue, . . .
> And dull, unfeeling, barren ignorance
> Is made my jailer to attend on me.
> I am too old to fawn upon a nurse,
> Too far in years to be a pupil now.
> What is thy sentence then but speechless death. . . ."
>
> Shakespeare, *Richard the Second*

"Why did you come?" I asked and bent to catch her answer.

Her voice dropped, a flash of grief charred her glance. "I love my mother. I love my Vietnam. I very sad. I loss my Vietnam. I loss my home. I loss my family. But we decide, it ees better to die at sea than live under Communists."

The immigration officer arrived, a Vietnamese who had been a refugee and had returned to Singapore to help his people in the resettlement process. Hurriedly, I took a piece of paper, wrote my name and address on it, and on the back the words WE WILL SPONSOR, and handed it to her. Mentally, I began converting the family room into a dormitory with space for five people.

Someone wanted a picture. We stood together, and she slipped her hand around my waist.

I have never been held so tightly by a stranger.

"Thank you," she whispered. "Thank you for your kindness."

I was stunned. My kindness? What kindness? It was she who was overwhelming me.

Taking my pause for misunderstanding, she persisted. "You know kindness? Here, I will write." In my notebook she wrote it, in big block letters. KINDNESS.

Did I? Did I know kindness?

The family groups began to leave, boarding the immigration crafts that had come alongside. My friend and her brothers and sisters were among the last to go. She stood beside me, her arm tight around me. I had the feeling that she felt secure here among the known, the defined parameters of this familiar ship. She was reluctant for that moment to leave, forcing her to face the next step of the irrevocable journey she had begun. Yet she alone was family head. She smiled at me, but her fingers nervously worked the corner of the paper I had given her.

Finally, the last boat arrived. The last group started down the ladder. "Oh, wait," I cried, thinking of one thing more. "When did you leave Vietnam?"

"I will write it for you." She smiled. She scribbled in my notebook, then hurried down the steps, carrying no possessions in her hands. The immigration boat sped away.

We waved. Farewell. *Farewell.*

She waved.

Oh, please, I pleaded inwardly. *Fare well.*

Emotion boarded the *Acuna*. I looked about. We were all wiping tears. Even the crew.

As I watched the immigration boat fade into the distance, I realized that this girl had touched a part of me I generally refuse to acknowledge. Though I had home and motherland to return to, in the deepest part of me, I, too, am displaced, a wanderer. In the core of my being, I am alone, alienated. In this hazard world, I hold refugee status.

We humans have common longings. We are the same. At some time, each searches for a hiding place, a sanctuary that will shelter life, that will let us laugh and sing. We hunt for a place where we will have room to become all we hope to be.

I knew I was not so different from this Vietnamese woman.

It wasn't until I returned to my hotel room that I discovered she hadn't written the day of her departure from Vietnam. She had written the date that they had been lifted from the waters of the South China Sea to the deck of the *Acuna*. To her it was the more momentous event.

18:30. MARCH 10, 1980. My father-in-law's birthday.

2   Mythic Moments
Wheaton, Illinois, March, 1960

I met my father-in-law for the first time on his birthday one warm March evening twenty-some years ago. My parents' home was only a block up the hill, and I had frequently walked past their house while running errands. Piano music had often floated through the open windows. My younger sister had even delivered their newspaper. But this celebration was my introduction to the hale and robust man and his complex and beautiful wife, two whose lives would soon become intricately bound with mine.

David had wisely taken precautions. Knowing that newcomers to his family notoriously won hard-earned welcome, he had already introduced me to an aunt and uncle, who had fortunately pronounced blessing. Thus my entrance into the family was eased a little.

But then again, I was the last. Family welcomes often grow proficient with practice. Or perhaps they all thought it was time that David marry. The young man was, after all, out of college, had taken seminary training, had suffered a misplaced affair of the heart, and was now, once again, at home. Perhaps my welcome was simply a matter of expedient timing.

I remember bringing a silly birthday gift for that first meeting, a taffy apple coated with chopped nuts. Perhaps it was an inappropriate gesture for first meetings, but then I was barely seventeen. It seemed perfectly appropriate to me.

David walked me home after the birthday gathering, up the hill, past the wooded lot where my younger brother and sister seasonally risked their necks skidding sleds through the winter snow and around trees. Then as we arrived at my door he kissed me good night for the first time, not once but twice. I think he had been subconsciously waiting until after this time of first meeting, which we had just accomplished.

At any rate, he kissed me, then whispered, ''Now we both know,'' and left. The door closed, and I had the firm impression that without a word I was committed to something beyond my knowing. Something beyond my ever knowing, even now.

And we didn't know—not about one another or about families, the ones we came from or the one we were to create. Despite all effort, families are never totally known. At best, relationships within them are elusive; often they are tenuous. There are rare moments of deep intimacy, faint glimpses that fade and shift, murmurs that tantalize.

Families are primally bonded, unioned beyond the intellect, and for that reason they are not really known—not ever, not with the head at least. They are best understood with the instincts, the sentiments, the heart.

I am the eldest child in my family and the youngest in my husband's. I play both roles awkwardly. Often, it seems as though I am only pronouncing lines, rarely finding the ability to extemporize the deep things in my heart. I am not sensitive enough. I walk the stage panic-stricken. My costumes—the personal and professional ones—prohibit intimacy.

In a way, the theatre of family is too important to me. I can only handle overloads of emotion by sublimating most of them. This cowardly repression protects me from rejection. But it also jails my intents. Consequently, often because of my own lack, I am disappointed when we as a family don't function the way I feel we should.

Recently, I have been intrigued by mythic moments. A patriarch's birthday. A date of first meetings. A celebration of family. A boat bobbing helplessly at sea. A rescue ship whose name means meeting place. The patriarch's birthday again. These are all the elements of myth.

Mythic moments are incidents in life, common to all of us though we mostly ignore them, so laden with truth they almost overkill meaning. They are pregnant with reality, ripe-bellied women, grotesquely overdue for delivery.

Mythic moments knock at our inattention, part the fragile curtain of our illusion, demand by overstatement that we stare at truth.

Through the years I have come to realize that the practical human response when one encounters the mythic is to do obeisance, to bow. It is only in this genuflection that life can be held, honored, revered.

Why did reality shimmer in that Singaporean sunshine, refract over the deck, curl beneath the canvas shelter? What faint curtain was being parted? What was so moving in that halting interview on the deck of the *Acuna?*

Perhaps I will never fully understand the emotional whys of that weighty moment. But I am aware that whenever we stare through the tapestries that separate us from one another, whenever we finally see the elemental meaning of another life, our deepest feelings are stirred. Before us the drama of rescue and critical human need and courage and benevolence had all been enacted. We had seen. We had touched. We were moved.

I was also aware that nothing I understood, nothing I sensed intuitively or knew practically, could impel me to similar abandonment. To leave family, even these ones with whom I so often inadequately communicate, to leave them with the thought of never seeing them again was utterly impossible for me to imagine.

I am the progeny of my father's clan. When they moved geographically, they moved en masse. In the genetic part of me, in some hidden inherited substance, I am clannish. The choice of leaving my family, if forced upon me, holds the power to destroy me.

Can it alter the Asians even less, affirming as they do the mystique of the extended family? Will they not always be homeless, even when they find a home?

I had held the flesh. That small stranger's body had embraced me, hanging on tighter than it knew, her wordless grip speaking volumes. Her tautness became mine. Her grief bore down on my lungs. My tongue completed her sentences, filled out the missing words. For a moment, I spoke her thoughts, became her mouth. In those instants we had breathed together.

I became confessor and in things unsaid she unburdened her guilt: the guilt of parting, the guilt of abandonment, of turning her back. This was her survivor's requiescat, this awful longing for the ones who have been lost, left behind.

Something is disrupting her culture. Something indomitable and unyielding is impelling this flight. It is something I have not touched, nor has it pricked my fingers. Against this hard rock I have not bumped in the dark. Shins unskinned, toes unstubbed, I do not know it.

I put this unknowing on my tongue to see how it would taste in the days ahead.

3   Life Turns
Singapore, Malaysia, March 28, 1980

Back in my room in Singapore that evening I wrote letters to extended family members. One went something like this:

> I have spent the day in Singapore harbor on board the rescue ship, the *Acuna*. Fifty-four Vietnamese boat people were fished from the sea somewhere around the time we celebrated dad's birthday together. They have left everything, risked everything.
>
> Talking with them made me realize how impossible it would be for me to permanently leave any of the members of my family or of yours. I cannot understand what compels these people. I can only sense the horror behind it.
>
> I am aware, however, that we in families infrequently say to one another the things that are most important. Suddenly, life turns, and there is no more opportunity to say them. Love is unsaid.
>
> I realize I have never told you that I love you or how much I admire and respect you.
>
> How inadequate we are in finding the right words or in knowing when they have even been said. We are all like Fairy, the insane asylum inmate in John Patrick's play, *The Curious Savage*. She sighs, and a fellow inmate asks her why.
>
> "No one has said they love me this livelong day," Fairy explains. "Why, yes they have, Fairy," comes the response. "I heard Florence say it at the dinner table. . . . She said, 'Don't eat too fast, Fairy.' "
>
> "Was that saying she loved me?" Fairy inquired.
> "Of course," she was told. "People say it when they say, 'Take an umbrella, it's raining'—or 'Hurry back'—or even 'Watch out, you'll

break your neck.' There're hundreds of ways of wording it—you just have to listen for it, my dear.''

So please, eat your vegetables, carry your umbrella, get plenty of sleep and don't work too hard.

Love,
Karen

I knew that evening there would be no meeting of persons in our family, no knowing of one another in any real way, until I found the courage to say the words ''I love you''—until I shed this carelessness and uttered the difficult sounds that were in my heart.

Is it not sad that what we hold in our hands often has no meaning until we see it torn from the grasp of others?

III   The Sacred

1   A Matter of Imbalance
Chicago, Illinois, March 1967

Once, years ago in a restaurant, my attention was captured by a rowdy group of men in the next booth.

"You're just like me," said one of them to another, rather loudly. "Nothing is sacred to you."

I thought about his words then as I have thought about them many times since. I think about them now.

What? Nothing is sacred?

No hallowed hills? No high places filled with rites secret in their mystery? No fire on the altars? No awe?

Nothing sacred?

I have heard this expression many times. People pride themselves in using it. They are the secularists.

I noticed something strange about that man in the restaurant. I was a booth away, yet I could smell him. Oh, it wasn't an odor as such, something the nose detects and sorts. Perhaps it was pheromones, those small chemical aerosols abounding in the animal world, which emit messages between the species and which some scientists suspect may be a means for nonverbal communication between humankind as well. There was a wave of something from that man, and I didn't so much feel as smell it.

I noticed this strange aura around some of the Western guests at our hotel in Bangkok during the week we were inspecting the refugee camps in Thailand. At first I thought it was their arrogance contrasted in bas-relief by the gentle deference of the Thais.

But later in the trip, while we were in Kenya, the comments of a second-generation missionary explained what I felt. Upset by Western dominance, he commented, "We have no idea, no idea at all, what kind of physical power we emit. It overwhelms the third worlder." I wondered if these emissions were the same as those I had detected long ago in that restaurant in Chicago.

I remember the first time I was disturbed by such a presence. A staff member of a large downtown church had rushed us across Michigan Avenue to the nearest and quickest eating place possible: the coffee shop of a men's club. I had never before encountered such physical men. They took up more space than their bodies required. It was not a matter of size or strength, however. It was a matter of imbalance.

All of my life I have been surrounded by men who believe in sacred things. They raised me, taught me, wooed me, joined life with me. They are scholars, men of prayer, men of service. A little absentminded, sometimes they function more completely in the subjective world, the world of ideas, the internal domain. Modern pilgrims of the soul, they often forget to note whether they are cold in the snow or whether their stockings match.

They are different from those men in the club. They do not smell the same. I have never been afraid of them.

Something happens when the tripartite union of body and mind and spirit goes out of whack. The dominion of the physical rules. It stomps on the spiritual. It becomes meaty, beefy. It protrudes, interferes, projects itself. It emits an essence overwhelmingly of itself. Dogs bark. Women hunch. The peoples of the third world cringe.

I am still afraid when I meet a man like this. They are the ones who do not believe in the sacred. I am convinced that this type of person will eventually become involved in nonsacred acts. He is likely to cheerfully, carelessly destroy everything in which I believe.

For, to me, everything has the potential of sacredness: be it pain or death or the common rites of each day. Nothing is without meaning. Eating food with the people I love can be sacramental. We pause; we share from the common pot; we join deep thoughts or ordinary ones. Life is bitten. We chew the core of one another.

Sometimes, I am kitchen priest. I chop, break, knead, blend, prepare the eucharists that give wholeness and healing. A poem, which hangs in the kitchen, reminds me that my awe hallows the bread.

> Be gentle
>   when you touch bread.
>   Let it not lie
>   uncared for, unwanted.
>   So often bread
>   is taken for granted.
> There is so much beauty in bread—
> Beauty of sun and soil,

Beauty of patient toil.
Winds and rains have caressed it,
　　Christ often blessed it.
Be gentle
　　when you touch bread.

　　The very words I speak give life. This child is molded as much as anything by my tongue. The ritualistic chants—I love you, I am sorry, I want you—these are the spoken prayers poured daily upon my modern wilderness. This smoothing, this fingering, this patting, this handling—these are my phylacteries, my prayer shawls, my measured marches through the cloisters.
　　I am a sacramentalist.
　　I know we must learn to see the world as it is, not only as it seems to be. We must learn to identify the sudden surprising clatter of numinosity. If not, we will trample things which have no meaning to us. We will throw them away. And in the process, we will unknowingly discard the very things that support and sustain us.
　　Nothing will be sacred. We will have thrown it away, and the world with it.

2   Land of the Thai
Ubon, Thailand, March 30, 1980

During the week we spent inspecting the refugee camps in Thailand, we took the night train from Bangkok to Ubon, where there is a refugee camp outside the city. The station was dark and bustling with musty life. Ragged men pushed large baggage drays and hustled business. Saffron-robed monks passed in twos, coloring the predominate gray. Harassed women herded and organized and fussed at their families. The engine wheezed and unloaded steam from its bowels.

One blond roustabout, his rugged age dulled by the night, sat on the platform with each arm around a Thai girl. "Ey!" he shouted. "Oi ben travelin' this way fer years. Sure as 'ell glad Oi'm not going t'night!''

We soon understood why. The air-conditioned car was not functioning, so an antiquated sleeper had been hauled out of storage and hitched to the train. It was hot. Our host began to make apologies.

No problem. Why fuss over the lack of a little climate control? After all, wasn't I the one who teased certain of my friends about going from an air-conditioned house to an air-conditioned car to an air-conditioned office, then home again to a heated pool? Certainly comfort wasn't the purpose of our trip.

I was sure this was going to be a glorious journalist's adventure. The exotic atmosphere of Thailand would blow all night into our unshuttered staterooms. I have always loved open windows.

Besides, we had purchased small plastic sacks of luscious fruits at the market to take on the trip. Ever since Tom the vegetable man dealt his wares in the back alleys of my childhood neighborhood, I have been an addict. His free handouts—a fistful of cherries, a ripe nectarine—had hooked me for life. Oh, the endless drugs of Thailand: the tamarinds, pineapples, kiwi berries, pomelos, the small, moist melons!

I sat alone in my dusty, age-worn compartment gorging myself and watching as we slowly edged along the back, nightside of Bangkok. A creaky fan wobbled overhead. I peered into the shanties where families huddled companionably around the charcoal embers of a single fire. My nose marked the *klongs,* boat canals that smell of musk and sewer. A stranger stood in the aisle, smoking a local brand cigarette. Its aroma was fragrant, bitter.

33

With solitude and fresh fruit and a journey ahead, I was content.

The words of the roustabout, however, proved to be prophetic. Soon the porter came to make up the beds, and he closed the windows, explaining that this was a prevention against robbers. The tiny cubicle, despite its arthritic fan, became sweltering. I slipped down the narrow passageway into the last compartment and entered into my initiation rites with the squat toilet and the unpredictable motion of the train.

Upon returning, I discovered that a Thai gentleman had boarded at the last stop and had been assigned the empty bunk in my stateroom!

Larry Ward, the host of our traveling party, bailed me out of my awkward predicament. We exchanged places, and I slipped into the hot berth beneath that of his sleeping wife—with all Thailand passing unseen beyond our boarded windows.

Chawing mosquitoes woke me at 2:00 A.M. The regulation railway blanket was one grade above haircloth, but I tucked it around me—despite the warmth—yanking it over my head as protection against the insects. I knew that real sleep was gone. Waiting for morning, scratching and sweating, I thought about comfort.

At 5:30 A.M., I escaped to the passageway and peered at the land that lay in dawn's shadow. The porter was just unlatching the windows on the aisle, and I think I startled him. There it was: Thailand, in all its beauty. The misty, rising morning opened its thirsty mouth and lapped its first drink. It stretched its arms. Water buffalo ambled, grazing dry grass. Small boys, surprisingly awake, good-naturedly herded the buffalo. Lean dogs tagged after the small boys. All turned to stare at the passing train.

Workers drew water, lugged it homeward, their feet tracing the pencil footpaths. Farmhouses on stilts acted as soothsayers of the future's intent. The waters would come flooding, changing all Thai farmers into boatmen. For now, all was stalk and crumbling leaf and rattling stems. Only chilies, green from irrigation, promised fertility.

Crafty, these people and creatures, hurrying to use the cool day. Thailand heat in April, the dry season, is like an unwelcome blanket on an already too hot bed.

I stood in the corridor, being jostled back into the sleeper as my fellow passengers pressed past me on their way to the last compartment. I watched as rosy dawn blushed. *This is the morning world I love,* I thought. *Here are the open windows.* The train *rockety-ricked* on the tracks. *This is the land. It is a sacrament.*

Be blessed, I breathed. Receive the coming love play of the rains. Eagerly welcome the hot attention of the sun. Swallow, seed, and sprout. Then become pregnant with green. Be nurtured. Nourish.

The children are hungry: the Laos, the Khmers, the Vietnamese, the Thais.

Land that feeds is sacred.

3   The *Barrios*
Guatemala City, Guatemala, March, 1979

In 1979, before my trip to the refugee camps, I spent two weeks in Guatemala City. During that time I was invited to have dinner with an unusual family. The father, a doctor, was not present because he divides his time between two practices: one in a midwestern state, which helps to support the other in the *barrios,* the sprawling slums that sprang up overnight after an earthquake devastated Guatemala in 1976. Constructed piecemeal of wood, cardboard, and plastic sheeting, these slums most inadequately housed some two-hundred-ninety thousand dwellers at that time. They are still a grim reminder of the *terremoto.*

The doctor's family lives in Guatemala City, and he flies down periodically. He and his wife have ten children of their own, five of whom were adopted after their American parents were killed in an automobile accident.

She and I enjoyed little significant conversation that afternoon because the doctor's family had also taken into their home fifteen additional children in various stages of infancy. While treating patients in the slums, the doctor knew that certain young ones would never survive without adequate nourishment. Medicating them without feeding them was useless. Not content to let them die, he began bringing the severest cases home.

His wife and I bounced babies all afternoon, kept them happy, consoled and cajoled them.

When the older children arrived home from school, a regular orderly routine went into effect. Each took charge of a favored toddler. Consequently, some of the crawling, climbing, and squirming babies were removed from our laps. Soon five high chairs were drawn from the dining room wall. Freed from my holding and hugging responsibilities, I wandered into the kitchen and watched as two teenage girls began to scramble eggs.

Five plastic bowls were placed on the kitchen counter. Five members of the high-chair crew were bibbed and lifted into place. They waited patiently while the cooking went on in the next room. In amazement, I watched as what seemed like dozens of eggshells were broken.

"You're not going to feed all those eggs to those little children, are you?" I finally interjected.

The look the girls gave me said that I knew nothing about life.

The five bowls were filled with three or four scrambled eggs apiece and plunked on the five high-chair trays. Five glasses of milk were placed beside them. Not a child moved. No little fingers grabbed at the yellow mounds. Prayers were the signal. Five little heads bowed. Then the eating began.

Again I watched in amazement. I have raised four children successfully through the toddler passage. The high chair in our house is still frequently occupied by nephews or the children of friends. It is a rule that this age child is fed only on linoleum, or when a plastic sheet has been spread. Our dog instinctively sits beside the person who is the messiest eater. She is ecstatic when she sees the high chair put into place.

In all my years of mothering, this was the cleanest feeding I had ever witnessed. There were no messy particles in the hair, no gelatinous smears down the bib. Nothing was spilled on the tray or on the floor. There was no banging, no tipping of bowls, absolutely no throwing of food. The only activity was eating. Despite my dubious predictions, each small child ate his whole serving and drank his full portion of milk.

The teenagers' glances were correct. I had a great deal to learn about life.

The body has a long memory regarding starvation. When the necessary caloric intake drops below the daily level required to maintain energy, the body literally begins to feed upon itself. It cannibalizes its own fats, muscles, and tissues for fuel. If one survives, this physiological trauma is not soon forgotten. Starvation sets in when an individual loses about a third of his normal body weight. If this loss exceeds 40 percent, death is almost inevitable.

One-half billion people are suffering from some form of hunger. Approximately ten thousand die of starvation each week in Africa, Asia, and Latin America. This grim scenario might be halted if poor countries would become involved in revolutionizing their food production and if rich and poor countries alike would curtail their population increase. Finally a joint effort would have to be made by the developed countries of both the East and the West to provide food, money, and technical assistance to the poor. But few experts predict that any three of these essential criteria will occur.

In 1951 the United Nations convention precisely defined a refugee as a person who, owing to well-founded fear of being persecuted for reasons of race, religion, nationality, membership of a particular social group or political opinion, is outside the country of his nationality or habitual residence and is unwilling to return. This technical definition doesn't include the hundreds of thousands of displaced persons who have abandoned their homelands because of drought and famine. Realistically, they are refugees as well.

Recent estimates state that there are a total of 18,000,000 refugees, the highest number since the Second World War. Most are found in Africa, the Middle East, Asia, and Latin America. Half of them are children.

There is a starvation that results from a lack of food, and there is a starvation that occurs from not having the right kinds of food. In other words, a full belly does not insure survival. A lack of essential amino acids can bring on kwashiorkor, a wasting disease that kills tens of thousands of the world's children each year. Those who survive are often marred for life. At least 80 percent of brain growth occurs between conception and the age of two. If the mother is malnourished, the fetus is starved. The brain of a hungry infant is inadequately fed. In many cases, mental development that does not transpire on schedule may not transpire at all. This kind of damage can be a lifetime incarceration.

The bowls were empty. There were no spills on the trays.

When one has been dying of hunger, undernourished cells demand feeding even when fat begins to form on the frame. A child slipping out from under the thin shadow of emaciation eats every particle of devourable food set before him. He is not certain of seeing food again. In horror, the body remembers eating itself. Nothing is wasted.

Deprivation can teach even the infant to revere the elements that give life. Food is sacred. A small child knows when to stand in awe.

There was no dog waiting beneath those high chairs.

4   The Milk Mixers of Ubon
Ubon, Thailand, March 31, 1980

After a night's train ride, we reached Ubon, Thailand. Ubon is a camp for Laotian refugees built in an old ammunition dump. Abandoned watchtowers guard the corners of this camp, and barbed wire marks the boundaries. But Ubon is really more of a village than a camp. An estimated five thousand to ten thousand have lived there over two years. Cottage industries have emerged. Women weave lengths of cloth on wooden looms. Sewing machines busily manufacture garments.

We toured piggeries and poultry projects and agricultural plots. Hut-front restaurants served homemade soup and soda pop. Refugees had even planted flowers outside their thatch-sided homes. Landscaping always indicates some disposition to permanence.

One morning I followed after Nan, the nineteen-year-old volunteer worker who was in charge of the milk distribution in this section of Ubon. Food rations are apportioned by umbrella organizations such as UNHCR (United Nations High Commissioner for Refugees), but supplementary feedings are often the responsibility of small voluntary agencies—"volags" in relief language. These agencies specialize in caring for pregnant and lactating mothers, children under certain ages or in malnourished states, and the elderly.

Workers were already about their business when we arrived at the Food for the Hungry distribution center. Vats of water steamed over open wood fires in one corner of the concrete block, screen-enclosed, cement-floor building. Young Laotian men and women laughed and flirted as the powder was poured and mixed, then strained to remove foreign particles, then stirred and strained and stirred again. A very sterilized potion was being prepared for the children of Ubon.

Then the children themselves began arriving. Many hefted younger siblings on their hips. They crowded at the doorways, pressed their noses and foreheads against the screening, peered at the activity. They were barefoot, often ragged, but none looked as though they were at death's door due to starvation. Credit for this goes to the daily feeding programs, such as the one I was inspecting.

Seven hundred plastic cups were placed on a wooden serving table.

Then the warm milk with most of the foam skimmed from the top, but with a little inviting froth remaining, was poured into the waiting glasses.

A more or less orderly line formed at the door. Serving was about to begin. One of the workers placed filled cups on the slender railing beside the table. Her lithe hands moved with innate grace. (They say the Thai women stretch their fingers periodically in warm water to make them more supple.)

Clup. Two glasses on the rail.

Clup. Two more.

Again and again the soft sound was heard. *Clup. Clup.* It was the cadence. Her hands were the motion. The act had become a dance.

The children moved through the door, took a cup of milk, grabbed a piece of protein candy from the tin at the end of the table, and then walked into the next room where they drank. The empty container was tossed into a large basket, and the drinkers exited, all with foamy mustaches on their upper lips.

"Would you like to serve?" Nan asked me.

I walked to the railing and looked out over the sea of heads and faces. The line of children pressed forward. The rail emptied. I moved to the end of the table and began the process myself, conscious that my hands were not nearly as graceful as those of my partner.

Two glasses. One for this boy with the tattered T-shirt reading LOVE YA. One for the little brother riding beneath his arm.

Two glasses. One for the barefoot girl child and one for the toddler clasping her hand. Two glasses.

A young mother passed, carrying her firstborn, both with finely etched bodies. She made a slight motion; he immediately pressed his hands together in the traditional Oriental greeting, the *wai*. Palms meeting, fingers extended, he touched his forehead to them. I bow to that of God which is within you, it means.

Another motion from the mother. He performed. He waved in the Western fashion.

Another signal. He said, "Thank you."

We all laughed. The mother and I smiled at each other. We had no common words, only common mothering.

I noticed that familiar faces began to reappear.

"The children may come back as often as they want," Nan explained.

The line moved. The railing emptied. Someone supplied freshly washed glasses. Someone poured the warm milk. We again filled the rail.

Two cups, one for you and one for you. Warm milk froth. Feet shuffling, bare feet on bare earth, then up onto the concrete pad. Heads moving in and out of position. Little hands receiving the glasses. Smiles indicating thanks.

The fragile curtain of my illusion shifted. I could see the sacred. It had become real.

I was among the milk mixers of Ubon who were whisking the raw sugar and the powdered protein. They sat and stirred, then strained five barrels of powdered milk and poured in the hot, boiling water, whisking and whisking, skimming the foam, ladling powder so the children could drink the milk, warm and sweet.

This is a sacristy, this place, which stores bags of powdered milk and kilns and pans and plastic glasses. These are holy things, ceremonial tools. And I, standing at the railing in front of these workers, am pronouncing blessing upon these children. This liquid, this candy are impanations. There is holiness in the giving of them, the receiving of them. They are the elements of life.

We are all communicants at this common railing.

Behind me, the workers began to clean the floor, the pots, the wire whisks. Water was poured to wash away the foam, the spilled powder. Brooms began brushing. Figures were marked in chalk on the blackboard, which daily charted the number who had been fed. We made preparations to walk across the way to visit the maternity-gynecological offices operated by another organization. The children dwindled. Turning, I looked back at the distribution center. A little child caught my eye, lavished a smile on me, then bolted, overcome by her own boldness.

By receiving this milk, they had pronounced blessing upon me.

Those who say there is nothing sacred have never fed hungry children. They have not heard the whisking wires beating circles in the boiling water and foaming milk. They have never heard the laughter of the workers, or seen the children pressing in line, seven hundred of them waiting to drink.

They have not placed cups of milk, warm and sweet, at the railing. They do not know that whatever increases the humanity of another is a holy act, and whatever decreases it is unholy.

Those who will not stand in awe have never had hungry children. They do not know the raw agony of starvation. They do not know the panting lethargy of empty bellies. They cannot understand the wonder in a tin of grain, a half-filled measure of rice, a cup of milk. They do not know this awe.

If the world ever turns, if there comes a time when their own child's joints poke through the skin, when its eyes hang huge, luminous and imploring, may there be milk mixers to feed their hungry ones.

We are all communicants at this common railing.

A full stomach says:
> A ripe guava has worms.

An empty stomach says:
> Let me see.

Creole Proverb

"Traveling in India we could toss banana peels out of the bus window without concern for littering. Momentarily a goat or a cow would wander past and dispose of the peel in a single gulp.

"One day two small children retrieved the banana peels our family discarded. The girl, about eight years old, wore a ragged saree. Her little brother of four or five was clad only in an oversize shirt. They were not beggars but watched for banana peels because they saw me coming from the fruit stand. As four peelings landed on the dusty road the children pounced.

"The girl brushed dirt from the peels. She handed all the peelings to her brother, pulled a grimy square cloth from the folds of her saree, and smoothed it out carefully beside the road. She and the boy sat down.

"Meticulously, the girl pulled the soft portion of each banana peel away from the outer skin and placed it on the cloth. The outer tough portions she tossed aside. She gave half to her brother. They began to eat.

"Whoever says that hungry people eat like animals when they have the chance did not see that Indian girl serve banana peels to her brother."

LaVonne Platt
More with Less Cookbook

IV   The Longing for Home

1   A Senator Still
Chicago, Illinois, August, 1980

In 1968 Marta Gabre-Tsadick was the first woman appointed to the Ethiopian Senate by Emperor Haile Selassie. Before that appointment she had served as director general of the Ministry of Foreign Affairs. One department beneath her direct authority issued passports, visas, naturalization papers, and resident permits.

By some quirk of favor she also found herself involved in the protocol responsibilities of receiving European and African dignitaries. She consequently became a woman familiar with heads of state.

In the 1970s, a severe drought led to widespread food shortages in Ethiopia. Thousands of people died of starvation. Demonstrations, strikes, and an army mutiny wobbled the throne. In September of 1974, a military junta, leftist in its leanings, toppled the emperor. Eleven months later, Marta and her husband were warned that their names were listed for arrest. Wearing only the clothes on their backs, they left their home, looking as though they were taking their two sons for an afternoon swimming picnic.

One highway runs from the capital of Ethiopia, Addis Ababa, to Nairobi, the capital of nearby Kenya. It is utterly desolate, aiming its way through arid wilderness without the rest stops and emergency centers we depend upon here in the States. Most people travel it equipped with spare parts and water jugs and survival gear. To escape detection, Marta and her family avoided this lonely paved road, winding instead through the trackless, sunbaked lowlands. Because they had little extra food or water and a child who was seriously ill with hepatitis, their concern mounted. Then as they were struggling against the rough terrain, their car broke down.

Death breathed on them. It became a near companion before they ever reached their first country of asylum.

Now in exile in the United States, Marta is tenderhearted regarding the refugee. She has been one. Her vision is often unerringly clear-eyed.

I am always glad to see my country through Marta's eyes. "Do you realize . . ." she often begins, then proceeds to point to a wonderful peculiarity of my people, which I casually take for granted. "I recently was shopping. And the saleswoman actually told me I could purchase the same brand item at another store more cheaply. . . . Do you realize how honest?

48

Where else in the world would you find people so honest as this?"

Marta carries herself like a stateswoman. She moves with quiet, refined grace. Her abundant black hair is piled upon her head, and in my mind I can see her walking comfortably through courts and council chambers with the greatest of ease. But she is not the least imperious, at least not now. She is ingratiating, without being condescending, concerned, and sincere. She wears a humility that is disarming. It cloaks her tall beauty, making her even more quietly beautiful.

"The government of your country is now Marxist," I once commented, seeking clarification. "Isn't that correct?"

There is no sarcasm in Marta. "What is the difference between Marxist and Communist?" she asks gently, seeking truth. "Do you know the difference? I myself do not know. It seems to me this is how it always begins. At first they are Marxist, then . . ."

Marta always shifts the curtains of my illusion for me. Her experience brings practical, wide-eyed clarity. One tends to think simply when one loses one's country. Either one has a fatherland or one doesn't. The issue is elemental. There is little of the vague, misty-minded pros and cons that fog the vision of those of us who struggle valiantly to be fair.

I am rapidly losing my liberality because of the Martas of my encounters.

Marta still strives to help her people, the Ethiopian refugees now huddled by the hundreds of thousands, starving and suffering in neighboring countries, Somalia, Sudan, Djibouti, Kenya. If the world was aghast at the Kampuchean crises, it will stare again, gaping, at the fragile quality of life in the East Horn of Africa.

Marta's husband, while in Ethiopia, was in charge of developing small businesses and light industries. Part of his responsibility was to oversee the Ethiopian displays at world trade fairs. He now operates a small business here in the States, but a major portion of his efforts are channeled into the not-for-profit organization that has been incorporated to aid their people.

"Son," said Marta recently to her child who had worked for months to save funds for college. "I have a place for your money."

Another refugee student needed it for schooling. Because of his resident status, he was not qualified for loans, but the son was. The money was willingly given. Then Marta's son took out a loan to pay his own tuition.

"How is your family doing?" I inquired recently, knowing she had received trusted but surreptitious word regarding the extended family still in Ethiopia.

"They are doing badly," Marta replied. "Just as we expected. Their health is poor. The physical conditions are intolerable."

She explained how relieved she had been to be able to send a message back to them. The communication was this: Understand that the work we are doing is not for our own glory. It is for the sake of the people and for our Lord. This is his work. If harm should come to you because of it, please count it as joyful suffering for the sake of Christ.

Marta is not like I am. I am not steel enough to ask my loved ones to joyfully suffer. I am too foggy headed to understand sacrifice in terms of larger, worthier dimensions. It is Marta who is clear visioned, who has accepted the fact that her own life, indeed all life, is only "temporary." Like any good government official, she has put the needs of her people before her own and those of her family. The refugee knows the importance of family and, paradoxically, the pressing priorities that come before family as well.

Though in exile, Marta is a senator still.

2   Outcasts from Eden
Chicago, Illinois, October, 1980

Early one morning, after I returned from the journey, I met Marta Gabre-Tsadick at O'Hare Airport and acted as chauffeur and guide while she gathered travel visas from foreign consulates in Chicago. By sheer persistent effort, she and her colleagues were able to persuade the powers that be to increase the quota of Ethiopian refugees allowed to enter our country.

In the process of seeking sponsors and funds to help her people to resettle, she had become convinced that she needed to travel to the countries of first asylum to see her people's condition firsthand and hopefully set up some organizations to care for them.

While Marta hassled with duplicate forms, I hassled with parking places. Finally, I found a metered spot that guaranteed me one-half hour for a quarter. Quickly I rushed her from the Swedish consulate to the French, which was scheduled to close within my rented thirty minutes.

In conversation earlier that morning, Marta had told me how generous the French had been in accepting Ethiopian refugees. The young woman at the visa counter, however, was unaware of all this. She refused Marta's own request to enter France.

"But I just want a transit visa," Marta explained. She needed to spend a day in France in order to procure papers that would allow her to enter Africa.

Marta is without a passport. She has a permit to reenter the United States, issued through the Immigration and Naturalization Service. Disbelieving, because other countries had been so hospitable, Marta pressed. We were taken to a superior, another young woman. She adamantly insisted that the regulations were clear and firm: No one was allowed to enter her country without a passport. If my friend was an Ethiopian citizen, it followed that she must obtain an Ethiopian passport. France did not recognize reentry permits.

Marta pressed again, throwing significant glances in my direction. Patiently she explained. It was impossible. The present Ethiopian regime would not recognize her. Nor would she accept a passport from the present regime.

She did not recognize it.

The third refusal was as firm as the other two.

Marta spoke again, attempting to draw some empathic hearing, "But you don't understand. I do not have a passport. I am stateless."

Stateless.

The word rolled; it tolled a quiet, doomed chant. I had never heard it spoken aloud before. It was a pronouncement of sentence, an admission of being cast out, cut off. State less . . . state less. . . .

No matter how far I travel, no matter what wonderful things I see or learn across the world, I am always eager to return home. I expect a welcome at U.S. Customs. If the officials fail at greeting, I remind them, "Aren't you even going to welcome me home?" Then I cheekily stand my ground until they perform an essential service I personally have included in their job description!

Last summer, after vacationing in the mountains of North Carolina, I plowed through all four of the lyrical, impassioned, often ponderous, novels written by Thomas Wolfe, who was born and raised in Asheville. *You Can't Go Home Again* is the title of his last book and is often quoted when people justify man's wanderings: ". . . for as you know, Thomas Wolfe has said that you can't go home again." Actually, Wolfe's autobiographical fiction was so thinly veiled, so devastating in its characterizations of real people, that he made it impossible for himself to go home.

Basically I think he is dead wrong.

I am of the opinion that the longing for home lurks hidden in the heart of every man. In one way or another we have to go home in order to be whole. One doesn't need to move geographically, one only needs to travel emotionally. We must reconcile our past with our present in order to prevent future internal division. This kind of schizophrenia is psychological exile. If we can't go home, even just to visit, to kick off our shoes; if we can't look the old place over and at least muse, "Well, it's not so great, but it's not so bad either"; then we are forever, uncomfortably displaced. Emotionally, we need a going-back place.

In one way or another, I suppose we are continually going home. Wolfe certainly did. His four massive volumes were poignant attempts at reconciliation. Rejection and carelessness and neglect. These are the threads. Wolfe's entire lifework demonstrated the struggle to go home.

For we must go back in order to understand who it is we have become and why. We go home to discover our roots, home to evoke memory, home to juxtapose our patterns of child rearing against what we want and what we don't want. We go home to die.

My husband's family bought burial plots in the old town cemetery one sunny, cold spring day after my trip. As the ancient caretaker marked out the eight spaces and my brother-in-law negotiated the planting of a tree over the resting places, I thought about going home.

In this cemetery the Memorial Day parade always ends. The war veterans and the boy scouts carry flags; proper words are said, and a makeshift band toots tunes.

Here as teenagers, we waited many a Halloween night for the inevitable scavenger hunters, who we were determined to scare by hollering through a vacuum-cleaner tube. Here the headstones, some crumbling and some askew from freeze and thaw, bear familiar names. Here I will finally sleep with my husband's family.

I am living once again on the edge of my hometown, a place I once declared I would never want to live again. I am becoming reconciled. I love the midwestern fields in spring when life burgeons. I love the frank, unadorned prairie downtowns, the tracks that carry grain and produce and products into the city, the train that wails at night. I love the grasshoppers' clicking and whirring in the tall July corn, which will stretch to man's height by August. I listen to the harmony of summer locusts and am exhilarated by the dusty rose, burnished bronze leaves of the great fall oaks. I love the difficult cold, the somber silence after snowfall, the testing and bitter endurance it represents.

The past rises in the faces of my parents' friends, now aging, in the teachers I meet who vaguely remember me being one of their hundreds of students, of the school classmates who call me by my maiden name. I wonder at the strange tenderness this evokes in me.

I am finally becoming at home in the emotional terrain of my hometown. It is familiar territory: trodden, well-loved, a native habitation, a returning place after wandering far and exploring frightening paths. It is a healing.

It is my friend Marta who cannot go home. Marta is stateless.

That seems to me to be a blow so deep one cannot understand it rationally. It is subliminal. To never hear the words, *"Welcome home."* To never be able to visit. To be a wanderer, homeless, estranged. To be outside the gates—expelled, dispossessed, unhoused. To not have the security of carrying one's own national passport. Marta, the former senator, once head of the Bureau of Foreign Affairs, which issued visas, passports, resident permits, and naturalizations, is stateless.

It is ironic. Marta cannot go home.

And yet in some ways we are all Martas. It is not going back home that is the problem, it is *feeling* at home.

"There's no place like home," we say after returning from vacations; a few days pass and the old restlessness returns unbidden. We begin to figure the cost of adding another room, though our house is large enough, or we replace the carpeting, though it has years of wear ahead of it. We long again for the beaches or for the mountains.

"Hills are the earth's gesture of despair for the unreachable," writes the poet Rabindranath Tagore. There is a part of every human that is displaced, a seed within each of us that germinates with inexplicable longings.

We long for perfect loves, for new and just societies, for security and order, for a place of permanent belonging. This desire fills our literature. One of the first books in Western literature that described a faultless world was Plato's *Republic* written around 375 B.C. All the Arthurian legends evoke the hidden desire for perfection. The very name, Camelot, indicates the bittersweet pattern of promise and lost dreams.

The work we generally associate with this theme is Thomas More's *Utopia*. It was published in Latin in 1516 and translated into English in 1551—sixteen years after the execution of its author at the order of King Henry VIII. It is the fictional report of a sailor who made three voyages to America with the explorer Amerigo Vespucci and tells of his travels through wild and unexplored regions. The greatest wonder is the island of Utopia, where all the men are equal, prosperous, educated, and wise.

The title of that book has become synonymous with all the perfect places for which we long. The dictionary defines *utopia* as being "a place of ideal perfection especially in laws, government and social conditions." And yet, the name *utopia* comes from the Greek words *ou* and *topos*, meaning no place. Though we long for it with all our hearts, though 18 million people in the world are hunting for it in one way or another, Utopia is no place.

We consequently become resigned. We sigh, and explain to one another, "There are no perfect people, no perfect places, no perfect systems." We accept what we cannot change, even accept what little we could change if only we would. The realization that there is no perfect place, that we will never feel at home, is the basis for our contemporary despair. But the old longings still lurk hidden though we have tried to forget. They raise their unwelcome faces at the first scratch of the surface—a new politician with promises, the communal movement of the 1960s—and we hope again. The hope is once again dashed and we sigh, "There are no perfect places, no perfect people. Nothing is perfect."

Our souls are wanderers, never really at home, though we go back home. We are the displaced peoples of earth, filled with common longings. We are haunted with desire. We are all outcasts from Eden, and we have never forgotten. Perhaps the particular genius of Christ is revealed in some of his last words, "I go to prepare a place for you. . . ."

We, like Marta, are ultimately homeless. Earth cannot satisfy us. We are ever alien.

3   Welcome Home
Thailand, Good Friday, 1980

Refugees are not black and white as so many photojournalists would have us believe. They are recorded in shadows and gray tones in order to capture our emotions. Rather, color them brilliant. Even in the most crowded conditions of the camps, love and tenderness and joy came shouting at us. These surprising realities are hints to the fact that there is more to the refugee story than terror, fear, and despair.

On Good Friday we visited Songkhla, a camp on the coastal edge of Thailand that holds Vietnamese boat people until their resettlement. Despite the fact that 6,000 refugees were crowded into rows and rows of inadequate thatch-roofed longhouses, Songkhla shimmered by the sea. It was radiant with sunlight, the mica in the sand reflecting day. The people were adorned with sunshine as well. Despite their deprivation, their hand-me-downs shipped in bundles from other countries, despite their survival uniforms, they also glimmered.

One is always impressed with the joy in refugee camps. Under the circumstances, it is such an unexpected constant. The foreigner arrives and immediately a curious, laughing crowd gathers. They test your receptivity, and if you seem willing, unstamped letters are pressed into your hand. Your payment for simply agreeing to mail these letters is a joyous, moving sort of gratitude.

For these thin papers are frail links between this crowded, uncomfortable present and the uncertain future. They are messages to relatives and friends, who have survived the death journey and gone ahead.

When I think of refugee camps, I often think, incongruously, of a happy throng.

To a man, to a woman, the escape circuit of the boat people covers a hazardous odyssey. In Vietnam there is the stress of gathering funds undercover, of waiting nervously for departure, which can take as long as a year. Then there is the agony of escape itself, onto the boat, up the river to the sea's mouth. Because of the cramped space in small seacraft, there is certain starvation of some kind during the days on high water. There is drifting in international waters where oceangoing vessels refuse rescue. There is piracy. And finally, arrival in safety zones where freedom from further suffering is

56

not always ensured. But the odyssey is not over yet.

There is the long, dehumanizing resettlement process: waiting for months in crowded refugee camps where food is scarce and disease eager. Scant sponsors and the whim of receiving countries determine the future. A refugee is bundled and numbered and transported and assigned and crowded and ignored and disbelieved and shuffled and allotted and overlooked—all without any control over his own fate.

Why? Why endure this dehumanizing process?

Through the years I have learned that when there is an inordinate result, there is also a justifiable cause. The cause is directly proportionate to the magnitude of the result. The answer to this why is simple. Refugees endure this dehumanizing process to avoid a system even more dehumanizing. Let the cause speak for itself. The writings of the refugees are poignantly clear:

> Why should we leave our country? We wanted to live; our patriots wanted to live; we wanted to appeal to the peoples' charity in the world; please look at our lives, not only to those who fled from Vietnam but also to those who stayed back and who longed to leave. Vietnam today was a gigantic prison and all the Communists were the most cruel wardens in men's history. . . . We were led by an invisible hand; we had to live like robots of the new era; we had to follow what we did not believe, to praise what we always despised. The police regime was applied everywhere. Nothing belonged to us: housing, dependents, and even ourselves. We were even more enslaved than all the slaves.
>
> Vietnamese refugee, "a witness"

My interpreter in Songkhla camp that Good Friday was a young woman who had taught English on the high school level in Vietnam. She had fled with her husband, a philosophy teacher, their child, and his brother and sister. Their little boat had been robbed twenty-nine times by pirates. One Thai pirate had finally kidnapped the sister. Two weeks later, she had escaped from him by running through the marketplace of a strange town shouting, "Vietnamese! Vietnamese! Help me! Help me!" By some rare quirk of miraculous fortune the family had been reunited in this camp.

The most precious possession a refugee has is not the gold bar to which all his fortune may have been reduced, but the address of a contact who will sponsor him in some receiving country. Before the pirates seized their ship, my interpreter had stuffed this invaluable scrap of paper into a bottle, which she then tossed casually into a corner of the jammed seacraft. The pirates threw everything into the sea that they didn't keep for themselves. Over the side went diplomas, certificates, important documents—everything but the ignominious bottle holding its precious, vital link to the future.

Because of my interpreter's excellent English, I conducted interviews in her and her husband's cramped, allotted space in the longhouse. The inevitable curious refugees crowded, peering, catching glimpses, overhearing snatches of conversation. The flies buzzed and the heat warmed us.

"Life is easy for refugees who arrive with something in hand," my interpreter and her husband told me. "Here as elsewhere there are those who have and those who don't have."

The two of them were among those who had been impoverished by the traumas at sea. Still they maintained their great good humor. Overnight, they became bean sprout farmers, scratching out some minimal subsistence by selling their produce at the flourishing market, allowed to exist just outside the camp.

At noon, our group left the camp to catch a meal, signing ourselves out at the commandant's headquarters as we had signed ourselves in. A huddled group of refugees, newly arrived but with some immigration difficulty had been dumped in the office. They were disconsolate, grim-faced. I risked a smile. A young woman responded in kind, but weakly. I had visions of them being consigned forever to this no-man's-land of eternally waiting.

Waiting. How one learns to wait in the camps.

Aleksandr I. Solzhenitsyn in *The Gulag Archipelago, I–II*, in "The Soul and Barbed Wire," actually gives thanks for the labor prisons because they give the gift of time: time to think, time to finish the complete circuit of one idea, time to taste the knowledge that years stretch ahead, time unhurried, time uninterrupted except by death. Time unmovable.

"Once upon a time you were sharply intolerant," he writes. "You were constantly in a rush. And you were constantly short of time. And now you have time with interest. You are surfeited with it, with its months and years, behind you and ahead of you—and a beneficial calming fluid pours through your blood vessels—patience.

"You are ascending . . ."

I have read all three volumes of *The Gulag Archipelago* and have little patience with those who decry reading about this experience because they "couldn't possibly stand it." If the world suffers, it deserves a hearing. If people go through these hells, I can at least read about it. Consequently, the refugee camps were familiar to me. Any crowded place that stores humanity against its will, no matter how humane it attempts to be, bears similarity to any other crowded place. A refugee, as well as a *zek* (a Russian prisoner), must learn to wait, must pace out the days that hold no profitable activity, must refuse the habit of sleeping too much, must guard against the inevitable mental lethargy.

After lunch, we returned to Songkhla, signing in again at the rude building that served as headquarters. The huddled family was still in the corner, their eyes big with observation. But someone had brought them a big bowl of rice and vegetables. Their spirits were noticeably lightened. So were my own. Someone knew kindness.

With my excellent interpreter, I spent the afternoon gathering further information, talking to boat people who had been rescued by the *Acuna,* one the older woman who had collapsed on deck after seeing her daughters ravished.

"You had a hard time coming out," I attempted sympathetically.

Pain pounded a sign in her eyes, which declared NO TRESPASSING. One brief glimpse at her naked agony warned me to tiptoe gently around this grief. I retreated and we talked with halting language about other topics. After a while joy sat again upon her gnarled face.

It wasn't long before I was seeking shady spots in the insistent afternoon sun. My purse was stuffed with addressed envelopes. It had become a mailbag. Suddenly, I felt overloaded. The heat, the stories, the gentle assertiveness, the loss of body space, which has become essential to me, a westerner, began to short-circuit me. Larry Ward was still busy making arrangements for the two new volunteer workers, who were being assigned to Songkhla. He needed to meet with a few other relief personnel.

My interpreter walked me to the fence, watched me slip through the barbed wire to the area beyond (where she was not allowed to go), and waved farewell. I walked to the commandant's quarters, signed myself out, then waited with the huddled refugee family in the shade of the old porch. Sitting together, we watched the camp wind down, dwindling in activity as the afternoon lengthened. I yawned. We were all feeling drowsy.

Suddenly, out of the corner of my eye, motion captured my languid attention. Down the road in the opposite direction of the camp, people were being unloaded from vans. They were obviously new arrivals. I watched and became amused at the officious young man, who was insisting on organizing them into twos, each properly spaced apart from the other. Nothing would do until his personal (and what appeared to me to be most unnecessary) sense of order had been satisfied.

Many were barefoot. All carried their sole possessions in their hands; most grasped four-corner-tied bundles. They seemed amazingly patient with the young man's idiocy. Their eyes were not on him, I noticed, as he pushed and prodded them into place. Their attention was focused on the camp.

Glancing back toward Songkhla, I did a classic double take, then glanced again. The fence, which had but a moment before framed a sleepy, afternoon refugee camp, was now jammed with people. More arrived with each moment, hurrying, crowding up against the wire barrier. Something rare and wonderful was forming. It drew me unconsciously to my feet and off of the porch.

Down the road, the officious young man finally gave the word, and the line of refugees he had so ridiculously formed into twos began to move. Two by two they marched, with the proper space between each duplicate quickly diminishing. Bare feet padded the dirt. Clutched bundles bounced. The pace quickened as they neared the fence. Smiles reflected light like the sand mica. It danced in their eyes, touched their mouths, brushed their hair. The sun, which had been so hot and unbearable only a moment before, was now a benediction.

The gate swung open, a little child catching a free ride on its motion. The crowd parted straight down the middle. A shout went out! A cry of welcome. A glad clamor of hello. The new arrivals, by now in total disorder, marched into the middle of the receiving committee. The throng folded behind them. They were swallowed by compatriots, countrymen, fellow survivors. The gate swung close, the same small lad riding it. In a little time, the sleepy afternoon returned.

I had seen a red carpet of human welcome. Instinctively, I knew it was an indelible moment. It was a familiar slice of celebration: the same moment of glory that swallows a victorious soccer team jogging off the playing field.

I realized I was holding my breath. I willed my lungs to relax.

I have a thing about welcome. It may even be inordinately important to me. Nevertheless, I believe in it. I think it is essential to human well-being. Because of our alienation, we are aided by it. Welcome heals.

I believe my children deserve to hear me exclaim when they rise each morning. They need to hear my words telling them how glad I am that they are home after a day of activity. My husband needs to be convinced of how deeply satisfied I am that he daily returns to me, how wonderful I feel about sharing bed and breath and bread with him.

I also ask that they return the same favors to me. It distresses me to find my way through a dark woods to my front door, to fumble at the black lock with my key because someone has forgotten to warm the night with a waiting porch light. I want shining paths to prevent me from groping. I want words that reassure me that I have been missed. I want someone to hold me after separation.

I want my family to know I am glad they are home. I want to know that they are glad I have returned as well.

Consequently, I know a welcome when I see it. The welcome in Songkhla, on Good Friday—death day—was a welcome of resurrection. It was a shout of beginning again, of having risked everything for the sake of something precious. It was the fellowship of suffering. It was fresh water after choking on ashes. It was joy yapping at the lagging feet of grief.

These new arrivals came out of the sea, having completed the circuit so familiar to those behind the gates. They came out of the jaws of dying, cheating annihilation, rising out of extinction.

They deserved their welcome.

And every human deserves welcome: the running, dancing feet of a little child; the hand grasp that speaks *Come here. Be close. Be near;* the warm smile when life's winter is barren. Even the embryo, unformed in the womb, deserves welcome, molded as it is by its mother's feelings. We need the light shining in the dark night, the bedroom glimmer that means someone has waited for our return.

And when we leave homeland—when we are torn and split

V   The Nativity

1   Grandpa's Children

Chicago, Illinois, the decades of 1960 and 1970

One of the finest acts I ever accomplished in my whole life was to give my father grandchildren.

After each baby, he would come to my hospital bed, strung out, ashen, gray. He had fainted after my birth and seemed near the same point after the advent of each grandchild.

During my adolescence—when the fainting incident was passing into the realm of family lore as we teased him about it—he always blamed my mother. She had so convinced him of her physical inability to have children that when mother and I survived the ordeal, he had no choice but to faint in dead relief. Mother always excused herself, casting blame upon her doctors, reminding us that they had warned her against childbearing because of her weakened heart.

My mother is a poet with a fertile imagination, which easily envisages the disastrous. Consequently, the labor and delivery process of any in our family is hard on her. We have learned to spare her as much anxiety as possible. My husband David, my brother, and my brother-in-law inform her of birth after all is done and accomplished.

Through the years, however, I began to also sympathize with the gray pallor on the face of my father. His mother had died of what my obstetrician guessed, at very long distance, to have been pernicious anemia. She couldn't keep anything in her stomach during a pregnancy and literally starved to death, carrying an unborn child to her grave and leaving two children—my father, aged five, and my aunt, aged three—motherless. Some say her death so altered my grandfather that his personality was never the same. It certainly breathed out of the past on my father.

I think each of our family births evoked a subtle, unadmitted terror in him. Though he never spoke of it, the actual possibilities were all too real. Soon my sensitivity stilled my orneriness. I refrained myself from teasing, "Now, daddy, I don't want you fainting on me, too." I came to recognize relief in the ash gray complexion, the white strain about his lips. I think he relived a little of his mother's death with each birth.

These hospital visits became familiar pilgrimages. Dad would appear at my door with the deportments of his workaday world of music tucked away.

The voice students and the practice rooms, the choral concerts and all the academia of his professorship were hushed. At that moment he was supremely and sublimely grandfather. Four times did he enact the visitation of the magi for me.

The gift he brought became familiar as well. He always carried a basket tray circled with dried fruits, shriveled apricots and pears, dates stuffed with walnuts, wrinkled prunes—all sealed in cellophane and purchased from some downtown vendor. I don't know why fruit seemed such an appropriate birth gift to him. I never asked. Loyalty taught me to enjoy.

My father never stopped to see me first. Primary reverence was due the infant, his infant. By the time he reached my side, the newborn had been predictably assessed, scrutinized, and evaluated. I knew exactly what pronouncements to expect; they were so repeated over the years.

"Sweet," he would begin, confidentially hunkering close lest his words insult whomever might be sharing my room (poor mother of some puny, ugly infant, no doubt!). "Sweet," he would start, then march outrageously through, "Prettiest baby I ever saw," and "Certainly a Burton baby," with frequent allusions to "our baby" sprinkled in between. My most tolerant husband might have contributed an ear or a nose but his side of the family never counted for much in the creative process.

Our first child was pretty battered by the birth procedure, but you would never have known it from talking to my father.

Daddy had always identified "our baby" in that nursery without the help of any hovering nurses. This was a simple task, because the infants always looked exactly like his own kids had looked. Of course. Without a doubt, they were the finest, the firmest, the most robust, the biggest, the smartest, the strongest, the handsomest, the most lively. On he would go, an intelligent and sensitive man, absolutely unabashed by his own pride.

Is there anything more wonderful for a new mother than the knowledge that someone you respect and admire thinks your children are more marvelous than you do yourself?

Only now, as an adult, can I look back and sense some of the courage that brought me into the world. I think both mother and dad chose nativity despite the risks. Consequently, because so much was risked, my sister and my brother and I were precious.

Because of my father's undaunted preening, there never were

grandchildren more chucked, held, cherished, doted upon, enjoyed. Daddy firmly believed in spoiling. There never could be such a thing as "too much love." Within two weeks of birth, he invariably, and in spite of infancy development norms, had the babies chortling. By this I am not referring to vague grimaces, which may or may not have been smiles. I mean enchanting infant laughter that drew the rest of us running from other rooms.

I've seen him do it hundreds of times, creep under the skin of a child, strike rare communication. Then off the two would go, chuckling together in a private, magical world.

My father inconvenienced himself to be with his grandchildren. They were invited on trips (even at troublesome ages), included on weekend excursions, snuggled down into his own bed on overnights. There were insane wrestling sessions in his house, wild hoop and holler chases, and touching—the amazing bounty of shared physical intimacies, holding and hugging and patting and kissing. I have a mental image of dad napping in the reclining rocker with a child sound asleep in his arms.

My father bought a retirement farm where he spent most of his weekends. Here, he molded warm memories for our offspring. The soft earth, plowed or planted, was part of his medium, as was the flooded creek, muddy and inviting. County fairs and garden pumpkins and the old barn groaning in the prairie wind—these were all a mix in the blend.

Dad could make any work an adventure: picking beans or gathering oily husked walnuts, collecting windfall apples or shaking the trees in order to have more. Once, he stripped clumps of elderberries from wild bushes, organized the children into crews, and spent one afternoon and evening pulling the tiny fruit into pans—staining hands and mouths and clothes all for the promise of homemade jelly. Mother and I had enough elderberry preserves from that one season to last for years.

How in the world did he make that marathon, boring task an adventure? The children, my children, who shrink and moan at the faint sight of work, stayed to the last berry!

Dad would borrow my children for a weekend in the country, offering slight excuses: "Going to plant the garden and need some extra hands," or "Lawn at the farm needs mowing. Sure could use some help with the tractor." Then he would return them in a mad rush on Monday morning, racing against traffic jams to reach his first class on time. They were never washed. He would dump them at my door, grimy and muddy and in a bliss of dust, perfectly content in their grandfather's love. My children's and my memories are filled with these mythic moments he created. Oh, that I could be the spinner of such memories for the grandchildren he never knew.

For my father is gone now. He is dead—I think. Yet he seems more urgently alive in some ways. And I mourn. Not for myself. (I am discovering how filled I am with my father.) But I grieve for my sister's and brother's children who will never know the full splendor of my father's personality.

I am incredibly grateful that David and I didn't wait for nativity.

My sister and brother, who are younger than myself, are now in the middle of the childbearing years. How frequently my mother says, "What would your father have thought about this new baby? Wouldn't Dick have enjoyed this child?" She and I know the answer to these questions. Separately, we are lonely for the extraordinary demonstrations of his love.

I try to fill the vacuum, knowing sadly that my efforts are not gifted. I make attempts at adoration, and, though I thrill at the familiarity that exists for brief moments between myself and my nephews—Brendan, Ryan, Justin, and Eric—I know that I am feeble in comparison. I am not the same as my father.

These little ones bounce on my bed, jumping up and down on "Aunt Karen's fowers" (the patterned bedspread). We make "bologna sandwiches." One piece of bread is plopped down (a pillow). A chunk of bologna (one small child) is plunked on top of it. Pickles and mustard and lettuce and an olive (much tickling and poking and probing) are pushed on top of the bologna. Then the whole concoction is topped with another piece of bread (the second pillow). After much hefting and hauling and bounding, the piece of meat (kicking and squealing and pleading for "more boney sanich") is finally dumped out of the pillows onto the bed.

These are special moments.

We hold and read and welcome, make annual trips to the zoo. But in our hearts we feel the loss. It is not the same. I cannot match my father's rare rapprochement. So I mourn that these little ones will never know his fervid admiration. Most men, I have discovered, are not like my father. At last I know it is not their fault. Daddy was gifted. His was a keenly hilarious, exuberant, deeply natural kind of loving.

In my heart, I know that these are not really my children, these nephews. Two belong to my sister. Two belong to my brother. This realization is perhaps where I fail.

For in my father's heart, despite all cautious rationale, my children were never mine or my husband's. In the deep instinctive part of him, he considered them to be his own. That was the subconscious message he acted out every moment he was with them—dragging the portable pool table out of the damp basement and setting it in the middle of mother's living room; teaching them how to play that most important of games, checkers; reading stories with extravagant inflection.

"Where are *our kids?* When are you going to bring *my babies* over?" was the slip of the tongue I heard so often but only understood recently.

That reality hidden in the heart of my father, I am convinced, is what made all the difference. It was the deep motivation that caused him, despite the risks, to celebrate nativity.

2   This Bent World
Cambodia, 1975-1979

In 1975 Cambodia was a country with a population of approximately 8 million people. As many as 4 million have died since then.

My mind boggles at the significance of this type of cataclysm. I think it is the numbers. That part of my brain, which sorts and sifts factor symbols, malfunctions. The black and white fact—4 million—moves me, but not in appropriate proportions. It is too journalistic, too matter-of-fact.

I can hardly absorb the newspaper pictures of stacked skeletons, skulls, and pieces of bones from massed graves that bespeak genocide.

The horror begins to shout in louder tones when I read the testimony of Phann Sophan, a twenty-five-year-old survivor who eventually worked in the camps for Food for the Hungry. A university student in Phnom Penh, the capital of Cambodia, he was a spectator to the mad rule of Pol Pot, head of the Cambodian Communist forces, the Khmer Rouge. For 3 ½ years, insanity reigned. The gentle fabric of life was disrupted in the most deliberate, unreasonable way.

Phann saw friends and relatives bludgeoned to death in open fields and tossed into shallow common graves. He witnessed platoons of Buddhist monks bayoneted as they knelt stoically in prayer.

Yet those are familiar tales. We are seared by the brutal realities of war and revolution. There is scarcely a survivor in any refugee camp in the world who is not haunted by brutal memories of death and blood and starvation.

But Phann saw the babies. Torn from the arms of their mothers, they were thrown into the air, caught on the ends of bayonets, bounced again up onto the points of knives and swords.

Now terror raises its head. I can feel it. It stinks about me. I am a mother, with mother instinct. I am fierce in my urge to protect.

Here pain creeps into my coldhearted insulation, which is born of distance and privilege. It lunges suddenly on me, a monster of unknown proportions. I hold onto the material of my fragile curtain lest I fall screaming into the abyss of evil that sits upon our world. I inhale and pull at air. I rage, "Oh, world! Why are you so bent?"

What kind of man can take a child, small and defenseless, with wide eyes and softness, and rape it? What kind of human tears an infant, round and

72

supple, smelling of milk, from its mother's nipple and tosses it in the air and catches it on the point of a bayonet?

The mother screams. Her voice rends the air. The miracle of nativity has been violated, destroyed by those who have long ago abandoned the sacred.

Keening, we weep, we mourn. Who will call down vengeance? Whenever, however, will amends be made? All the curtains of my sheltered existence hang jagged, dirtied with filth and blood. Terror is loosened to roll and fall among us.

Contain it. Hold it. Keep it from engorging itself upon us.

I weave prayers around my eight year old, the last to receive my father's blessing. *Keep him from evil men.*

I intone exorcisms above our family's infants, my father's babies. *In the name of the Father . . . and of the Son . . . and of the Holy Ghost. . . .*

Is there no help for us? No help at all? The world is warped. What keeps it from spinning off course, wobbling into other planets, the moon, the sun? Do these horrors lob it from its orbit?

We are not better than we ever were.

The Assyrians split the bellies of pregnant women as part of their conquering humiliation. Newborns were cracked upon the stone, their throats incised, their blood sprinkled on the altar. Then the cast-off body shell was discarded down the multitiered steps of the ziggurat.

Herod ordered the slaughter of the innocents.

Ivan the Terrible dispatched his own son with his own hands. He surrounded the rebel city of Novgorod and sat on a throne in the open air while for five weeks sixty thousand were tortured to death before his eyes.

The cattle cars, the gas chambers, the furnaces.

Life is fragile; it is fragile; it is very tender.

Now a new game, a grisly game has been invented. Infants are its victims.

Oh, world! We are weary. Something bent always raises its head. Carnage, calamity, chaos rule.

Where are the children? Count them. Draw them close. It rises unsuspected, takes advantage of our unguardedness. What will keep us all from sinking into this pit?

Dirge Without Music

I am not resigned to the shutting away of loving hearts in the hard ground.
So it is, and so it will be, for so it has been, time out of mind:
Into the darkness they go, the wise and the lovely. Crowned
With lilies and with laurel they go; but I am not resigned.

Lovers and thinkers, into the earth with you.
Be one with the dull, the indiscriminate dust.
A fragment of what you felt, of what you knew,
A formula, a phrase remains,—but the best is lost.

The answers quick and keen, the honest look, the laughter, the love,—
They are gone. They are gone to feed the roses. Elegant and curled
Is the blossom. Fragrant is the blossom. I know. But I do not approve.
More precious was the light in your eyes than all the roses in the world.

Down, down, down into the darkness of the grave
Gently they go, the beautiful, the tender, the kind;
Quietly they go, the intelligent, the witty, the brave.
I know. But I do not approve. And I am not resigned.

Edna St. Vincent Millay
Collected Poems

3   The Fissure Menders
Thailand, Easter Sunday, 1980

Goodness is the only answer to the depravity that infects our world. For the story of the refugee is also the story of the relief worker. These are the fissure menders who struggle to close the yawning chasms of evil. They are often a combination of unlikely temperaments, dispositions, and motivations. They are mostly unknown, unsung. A few are opportunists, siphoning funds and goods for illegal personal gain. Most are like the middle-aged Australian couple who sold their real estate business in order to finance themselves in the activity of salvaging humans.

Generally, the press thinks of them as being good for little more than a brief quote, but many are the source of utterly fascinating stories.

Most relief workers believe in something—either life or humanity or a God who impels acts of goodness. Something is sacred to them. They stitch quietly at the rents in the world.

I met Karen Norbeck and Billy Huber on Easter Sunday in the Thailand camps of Khao I Dang and Sa Kaeo, respectively. Both were American college students who were serving as student volunteers.

Four basic functions dominate the responsibility of relief personnel faced with this incredible surge of crises. Each category contributes to keeping the refugee alive. Obviously, the first is feeding and housing. The second is medicating and nursing. The third function contributes to the hope for the future by participating in the bureaucracy of resettlement or in the frustrating efforts of repatriation. The fourth is generally the last because the others are the wheels that squeak louder. It is to create hope for today by providing morale.

Karen and her colleagues were in charge of the first function, supplementary food feeding in the largest section, No. 5, of the camp. Khao I Dang has always been one of the most swollen of refugee settlements, housing a number over one hundred twenty thousand refugees who are mostly Cambodians. Section No. 5 was responsible for some twenty-four thousand of that population. The supplementary feeding provided one nutritionally balanced meal for pregnant and lactating mothers, for children under five, and for the elderly. Food for the Hungry had recently expanded the kitchen shed and storage rooms, built tables and stools, and purchased several thousand new enamel bowls for the feeding project.

The meal, which is fed to the mothers and children, usually consists of a high-protein dish made from chicken or pork, chopped cabbage, sweet potatoes, onions, bean sprouts, and mung beans. Fruit is often an additional complement as are protein crackers. In some camps, the refugees have been persuaded to substitute the healthier brown rice for the traditional white. Often refugees are employed to prepare and cook the meals, thereby gaining a small source of income. The day we arrived they were slicing gelatinated blood for pig-blood soup.

There is a lingo the children in the camps chant. "Ello," they sing. "Goot-bye," they shout. "Ou-are-yo," they call. After a while it becomes a dinging litany.

As the supplementary feeding was winding down, we toured much of this section of the camp, looked at the center that was to become a sewing room, walked into and around the flimsy thatch-roofed, bamboo-sided houses—with children always tagging behind.

I had become tired of responding hello, good-bye, and I am fine. I stopped. "Here, try this," I instructed. "Meet you in Amsterdam."

They mimicked. "Mit yo een Ahm-sta-dahm."

Such success! We tried again. "See you in Paris," I verbalized, drawing out the vowels.

They mimicked again. "Tsee yo een Paree."

By this time the gang had gathered, and we were having a fine time. Slightly overconfident about my linguistic abilities, I proceeded to teach them a song out of my Brownie Scout leader days—with motions. We began, as usual, off tune.

"Six little ducks that I once knew, fat ones, skinny ones, and fair ones, too . . ." In a little while, a hundred Cambodian children were singing, "Quack! Quack! Quack!" (the rather distinctive chorus of this piece) in a broad Khmer accent.

Joy in the camps! How quickly it startles one with its presence when it has no right, no right to be there at all.

Karen Norbeck (who had been bitten by a rabid dog soon after starting her assignment and whose initiation to volunteerism was therefore the rabies treatments) pulled a bottle of bubble solution from somewhere and began blowing rainbow spheres into the hot air. They soared, floating high above

76

our heads. The children danced, their bare feet hopping on the brown dirt alley. They laughed, chased the bubbles, and broke them. She swept more into the air, then gently more followed after the arc of her arm.

We toured the hospital wards, thatch-roofed, dirt-floored affairs crowded with metal cots and jammed with the extended family members or friends of each patient. The wife of one of the Christian refugee pastors, a Cambodian, had just given birth to their firstborn, a son. The father lifted him above the heads of the hospital crowd to meet our appraising examination. There was more than just paternal enthusiasm glistening in his eyes. *Here is life again,* the waving bundle in his uplifted hands proclaimed. Here is nativity daring this unhappy world.

One of the doctors was introduced to me as a heart specialist from Portland, Oregon, who was volunteering his services for a few months in the camp.

"How are you doing in all of this?" I questioned, motioning my head toward the overpopulated ward, but really wondering how on earth his training had helped him accommodate to the heat, inadequate supplies, and deaths from malnutrition and maltreatment, which are rarely seen in the antiseptic hospitals of the States.

His eyes misted with sudden, surprising tears. "It has changed my life," he answered as nurses hurried past us with trays of medicine. "For the first time, I'm practicing the kind of medicine I went to medical school to learn to practice."

Bubbles on Easter Sunday. Singing on the dusty paths. A new baby in the wards. How we need morale to leave death, to keep its cold hand from squeezing the heart.

Later that day we arrived at Sa Kaeo. Billy Huber, the other college volunteer, was just finishing a supplementary feeding. Large empty pots littered the cooking shed, their sides dripping perspiration as were we all. Billy daily stirred vegetables and meat bits in the great woks to serve thousands. I wondered how often he had helped in his mother's kitchen. . . .

Sa Kaeo is the camp that shelters those refugees belonging to the Khmer Rouge faction (the Cambodian, Chinese-backed Communist forces who were forced out of Cambodia when the Vietnamese Communist party came to power). Journalists dubbed it the death camp. At the beginning, a refrigerated body box cooled as many as fifty corpses per day. Pictures of this camp helped to rouse the conscience of the world.

Now many of the agencies are closing their hospital wards. A certain normalcy has returned; the medical problems are mostly ordinary ones. For the moment, grim crisis has pulled its dark hood about its face and waits in the jungle, the mountains, across the border.

One previous hospital ward had been turned into a cultural center. Handmade looms took up half the room; the other side was occupied by an industrious wood instrument orchestra and a choir in the middle of practice. The music master clapped rhythm, mesmerized attention, evoked the melody of thrumming wind chimes and luted voices. I stood in a shadowed corner and thought about the hum of looms, listened to the lifted lilt of singing, and remembered violent death.

How presumptuous life is, I mused. *How it pokes itself into places it has no business being.* The lines of a modern hymn came jabbing into this death place, now a place of life: "He came laughing and juggling out of the tomb."

I interviewed Karen and Billy several months later after we had all returned to the States and they had resumed their college classes. I was curious as to how young adults would sort this exposure to drastic societal disorder. Had they gone through culture shock? Did anyone at home seem interested in their experience? What were their plans for the future? What had been good about the whole adventure?

We sat at a table in the student lounge. Young people filled the room around us, immersed in conversation and studies and each other. Thailand was a semester away.

"The best thing about the camps was the people." They both agreed on this and expressed admiration over the ability of the refugee to smile for all his pain. They wondered at the way innocence, love, and gentleness had been preserved. Or perhaps, cataclysm had restored these qualities to a people from whom they were once lost.

"What do you miss?" I wondered.

Karen's eyes had been teary more than once during our discussion. I thought of the Easter Sunday bubbles floating above the waving hands of children.

She smiled and answered, "Thai food," then laughed, then became serious again. She missed the children. She missed holding the infants. She missed teaching in the camps.

Billy had brought a box of photographs. We looked through them, and he pointed to the face of a small child sitting in a huge cooking pot, his body hidden inside the container, his eyes pensively large. "I miss little guys like that."

Billy Huber is what some old-timer might call a strapping youth. Good-looking, his hair was not as blond in the midwestern autumn as it had seemed under the beating sun of Sa Kaeo, which turns many things golden. He leaned back in his chair in the student lounge and answered again, refining his point. "I miss the babies."

4   Compassion Fatigue
Indonesia, 1979

A few, a very few, of the relief workers who help in the refugee camps become saintlike. A great many others are actually wounded, even destroyed, by their own benefactions. They become swallowed up by the elemental distress, scorched by their long looks at unnatural, immense suffering. Many internalize the despair. Unknowingly, they put aside their needles, which work to mend human misery. Their capacity to be disturbed becomes blunted.

All these workers struggle against compassion fatigue. Weariness numbs the soul. The numbers alone boggle the heart. This condition is illustrated in the following excerpt from a letter written by Lynnell Mickelsen, who worked with the U.S. Refugee Program in Southeast Asia in 1979.

> Two months ago I was sleeping on my baggage in a small private airport, surrounded by 20 sleepy oil riggers who were baffled about what I was doing there at 7 a.m. (Answer: trying to hitch a ride on a Conoco flight back to Indonesia.) I woke up to find a man shaking me and saying, "Excuse me, but are you with the U.S. Refugee Program?"
>
> I nodded.
>
> "I'm from the United Nations. We have a package for you."
>
> I opened the package to find a hypodermic syringe, some tiny bottles and a telex from the embassy that read, "Please deliver this to Dr. Nguyen Truong Thanh at Kuku, Anambus. Baby suffering from (I don't remember the disease) and will die unless it receives medicine within 24 hours."
>
> I looked up and asked, "How do you suppose I get this to the Anambus?"
>
> He said, "I don't know. Doesn't the plane go up there?"
>
> "No. It drops me off at Tanjung Pinang and goes on to Matak, but that's still 100 miles from Anambus. The only way they could get in would be by chopper from Matak and this is Conoco—an oil company. They don't have to do this stuff. They only let me hitch to Tanjung Pinang out of charity."
>
> He shrugged, "I was just told to give it to you," and walked away.

I was frustrated. This is the kind of thing people often do—give impossible assignments to young field staffers and leave them without the resources to carry them out—often because they have no idea about the logistics involved. I got off the plane at Tanjung Pinang and handed the pilot the package and the telex.

"Listen," he said. "I'm only going to Matak."

"I know. But hand it to someone at Matak and if they can get a chopper to the Anambus—great."

"Young lady, do you know how much helicopters cost? $300 an hour and that's a two-hour trip. We're a business. We can't do this."

I said, "I know. And if you can do it, fine. If you can't, fine."

"What do you mean *fine?*" somebody interrupted. It was a new staff member. "How can you say 'fine, fine' when there is a human life involved? What is $600? If the medicine doesn't get there the baby will die."

I heard myself reply, "So what? What is one baby? Fifty babies probably died last month and no one sent them any helicopters. All they needed were some mosquito nets, malaria pills and milk for the mothers. What makes this baby so important? It's probably not even dying. Someone on a flying visit must have spotted it and freaked out."

I shrugged and walked to my car, leaving the pilot holding the package and his own moral dilemma. I learned a week later that Conoco had flown the package in by helicopter and the baby was saved. But my own reaction, an exasperated "What is one baby?" still bothers me, because I meant it.

Weeks later, still overburdened by the sorrow and futility that she was witnessing, Lynnell wrote another letter:

There is a Franciscan convent about five miles from my home. I sometimes hop a bus there. The grounds are quiet and one can sit alone for hours in their chapel. As I get older, I find myself drawn to places where I can kneel and fix my eyes upon a cross. It helps my mind. I sat in the chapel last night and thought, *I hurt in so many places, on so many levels and from so many things that I cannot list or explain them. I do not pray. I am tired of hearing my mind's attempt to say something meaningful or fitting. I am just going to kneel here because I need to be healed and cleansed.*

Ideas came and went. I thought about self-pity and how it usually comes when I feel misunderstood and alone. I thought also about how Christ was misunderstood and alone, how his crucifixion was a product of people's pride, hypocrisy, ambition—their lust for power. His executioners never felt they were part of a great cosmic battle between good and evil. Instead, the crucifixion of Christ was a petty, mean act carried out by men trying to protect their inane existence. Yet despite the shabby motivations of his executioners, the effect was devastating: Christ died.

"On the third day he rose again . . ." I say the creed every week until, through repetition, I forget the significance. But the point is that although the evil was strong enough to kill Christ, when put to the test good was stronger. The resurrection is physical proof that stupidity and hopelessness are not reality. Love is. And, as I type this, without husband or family or best friends, I cannot be loved more completely or intensely than I am being loved by Christ right now. My problem is, in the face of the suffering in the camps—when I can only say, "The horror, the horror"—I start thinking stupidity and hopelessness *are* reality, that evil really did win. And yet, I still must believe evil doesn't have the last word.

5   Jubilee
Hong Kong Island, March 26, 1980

Statistics again. Hong Kong, with a land area of only 404 square miles, has a population of more than 5 million. This amounts to an overall density of some 12,400 persons per square mile, double the density of Los Angeles, and far above the U.S. average of 62 persons per square mile. In Mongkok, one district of Hong Kong where refugee camps are located, the density mounts to 288,000 persons per square mile.

Hong Kong has long had to deal with the illegal immigrant escaping from mainland China. In one 22-month period during 1978 and 1979, there were 230,000 of these, representing an addition to the population of 4.8 percent.

In May of 1975, the first Vietnamese boat people began to arrive—3,743 came on board the *Clara Maersk*. That was just a foretaste of the wave that would splash and pound against the harbor city. In 1979, 72,000 Vietnamese immigrated. Considering the enormous problems of feeding and housing and medicating and processing all these refugees, Hong Kong is to be commended for her incredible open-door policy.

On the first leg of our journey we surveyed one of the Vietnamese refugee warehouses, Jubilee Camp, administered by the International Rescue Committee, IRC (the jargon of initials abounds in relief organizations). Youth with a Mission (YWM), a volunteer agency, was responsible for much of the daily functioning of the camp.

Jubilee had been a former police barracks, a multiconglomerate maze of grim concrete cubicles. Rising four floors high, it is an estimated one hundred fifty yards long. At the time of our visit, the population was around six thousand, down from eight thousand eight hundred a few months before.

An old bus was being converted into a child care center. We began our tour with it, then walked across the way into the communal kitchen of Jubilee itself, where several Vietnamese women were preparing vegetables. Our guide, the spokesman for YWM, explained how raw sewage had poured from the broken pipes overhead into the water drains. He told how his organization had undertaken a massive program of plumbing rehabilitation, repairing the drainage systems, installing functional latrines in the washrooms.

We turned to leave, following our spokesman. The women nodded to us, bent at the waist, smiled the smile of those to whom the spoken conversation has been undecipherable, the smile I smiled many times on this journey. It means goodwill to you, good intent. I caught myself bowing and nodding in return, then hurried behind the trailing voice of our guide. "Here the excrement was inches high, maybe a foot deep. We had to shovel it out."

The rooms were amazingly in order, considering that each family was allotted one bunk bed per family and several bunk beds were crowded into each cubicle. Blankets hanging over the sides provided privacy. We climbed to the roof and looked at the soft, wondrous view of Hong Kong. My mind envisioned pots of imaginary flowers blooming against the grim building. I planted mental vegetable plots beneath the sky.

We watched a little girl sliding down the steep roof, catching herself blithely before a sheer four-story drop. I thought about an emergency safety fence.

We descended the four flights of stairs, and I became separated from the group because I lingered to ask questions of the women workers in another crumbling gray cubicle. They were in the process of setting up a day school. Their crude wood table was set with books and crayons and paper. Both had sun-bleached hair and aquamarine eyes.

My daughter looks like this, shining and blonded. I thought about Melissa shoveling a foot of excrement, scrubbing the walls, wrestling with corroded and rusting pipes.

I could hear the muffled voices of my group somewhere in the maze ahead of me. But because of the labyrinth of twisting hallways, I opted for the nearest exit, rather than take a chance on losing my way. It was safer to wait for them by the entrance.

Suddenly, a little hand slipped itself into mine. I looked down into black eyes and black hair and the most shy of shy smiles, and teeth rotting from malnutrition. I thought about dentists.

My new escort walked with me past happy children risking their necks by catching a rubber-band jump rope with their feet. Another little girl sat on a small industrial spool, then shifted it on its side and propelled it along with her stomach. Eager boys aggressively jammed wooden circles on caromlike boards.

I was wearing brass bracelets, which were imported from India and had cost five dollars at Carson, Pirie, Scott & Co. in Chicago. Two young women eased up to me. Pointing to the bangles, they spoke confidentially. "Golt?" they inquired. "Golt?"

I laughed.

They laughed.

We bent at the waist.

No, they weren't gold, but I didn't know how to explain brass. "Brass," I ventured. "You know brass?"

"Brazs," they mimicked.

I had been right. They didn't understand. We shook our heads, shrugged our shoulders, lifted our helpless hands; all three of us performing tandem universal gestures.

Those bracelets were stolen along with a television, several antique clocks, the rest of my costume jewelry, and a few other odds and ends several months later when our home was robbed. I could scarcely find the heart to complain, though I enjoyed wearing some of the jewelry and I felt sentimental about the old clocks because my parents had given them to me. How could I justify one whim of self-pity when I had so recently seen people with nothing, those who were simply happy to be alive?

The group finally merged again. One man, who had joined us for this tour of Jubilee Camp, seemed noticeably subdued. Perhaps he had never been exposed to poverty. Due to ten years of work in the inner city, I was aware that there were physical deprivations much worse than this. As far as I was concerned Jubilee was cause for jubilation.

A small, still hand was folded in mine.

Women without words had smiled and nodded and bowed together.

The structure was crumbling but amazingly clean.

There was food and obviously someone from the world community cared. The refugees were allowed to come and go, to find jobs. The population was down, meaning that numbers were being resettled.

The children were happy.

Apart from needing geraniums potted on the roof and a safety shield and a dentist (which my host for the trip was able to cover out of a special emergency fund), things were not so bad in Jubilee.

With what a loud clamor the demon cat claws its victims. How it roars. Yet how quietly the needles of the fissure menders bind the wounds together.

6   Life Rises
Prasat, Thailand, April 2, 1980

Walk gently in Prasat, walk gently . . .

As camps go, Prasat, Thailand, is tiny, holding only some three thousand Khmer (Cambodian) people. Because of its size—or perhaps because we arrived on a sleepy afternoon during the week we were in Thailand or perhaps because the interminable sun was blessedly blanketed by rare Thai thunderheads—the refuge seemed a place of mourning, a tiny spot of corporate grieving, where three thousand were working through the stages of grief together.

Walk gently . . .

We drove through the camp to the pig barn, a work project sponsored by Food for the Hungry, past longhouses with corrugated metal roofs and sides. I thought about the interior of those houses: of family upon family in sectioned spaces, of a hot and sweltering Thailand afternoon. The corner of one house had been bent up to catch some breeze. It looked ever so much like the lid on a sardine can that someone had begun to roll back.

Men lounged in groups, some playing a game with small black balls. But there was none of the thronging, jammed atmosphere we had seen in other camps. The children were returning from what looked like school; many had books of some type in their hands.

The quiet of the sleepy camp hushed my own soul. Stilled, it began to examine the sad nuances of Prasat—three thousand people in corporate grief. Suddenly, Nancy and David Roberts appeared, married volunteers who had interrupted their college studies in the States to make themselves available in the refugee camps in Thailand. They were receiving an education of another kind. Nancy had never worked with pigs—now she and her husband were in charge of a piggery project.

Nancy has absorbed the sadness of the Khmers among whom she works, but it has not dampened her joy, only quieted it. She is a lover, one of those who spreads concern with natural ease. People trust it; they are drawn to it. Instinctively, with the flair of a storyteller, she shares the tales of the people she has come to respect and cherish.

The murmur of thunder puts an exclamation point to our conversation. Rain, a gentle miracle in this hot Thailand dry season, begins to fall. Sparse, it

86

is nevertheless a welcome mercy. We take shelter in a big barn, which houses feed and supplies, and we sit on a storage platform while David occupies himself with some business at hand. Consequently, I see Prasat through Nancy's love.

"You can talk to anyone," she explains. (She has found an interpreter for me.) "Everyone has a story."

So randomly, we begin with those who are in the pig barn. Pow and Nook are both sisters, widows who are working as pig farmers. They are from Batambong Province in Cambodia, and both are extremely shy. We sit together on the platform. The gentle rustle of rain on the roof is comforting. It matches the personality of Prasat. Thatch falls on our hair, on my notes. I brush it away.

Nook is thirty-one years old. Her husband was executed by the Khmer Rouge. Pow is forty. Her husband was taken away. She never saw him again.

I ask Nook the ages of her children. One is seventeen. One is five. I wonder about the gap of years between her children. This is an unsophisticated, provincial woman. That gap must speak a volume of misery.

We do not talk of the children who once filled that gap and, I suspect, are now dead. I leave her the dignity of private pain. These are women who are barely emerging from the dark shroud of death.

Our interpreter's name is Salee, a young man whose whole family has been murdered. He is only one.

"Oh!" says Nancy, suddenly remembering. Her eyes light with joy; her straight back straightens. "Salee has wonderful news! Salee has married a wife! And she is so beautiful!"

Nancy talks about the weddings in the camp, about people who have lost everyone finally finding someone to comfort and to love. Salee had once said to her, "If I die, if I'm sick at night, no one to take care of me."

Photographs are produced of Salee's wedding. His wife is exquisitely beautiful.

At the wedding the groom walked under an umbrella to meet his bride, and the men of the camp walked behind him. They came behind, the Khmer men who had lost family and whose manhood had been assaulted because they had been unable to protect their women or lay down their lives for their own children.

Nancy's voice goes on. "The need is so great. They marry because of the devastating loss and loneliness and because of mutual pain. Then love comes."

Some of the workers are called. They gather together. "You must hear them sing," says Nancy. A small girl is found to dance. The Khmers stand in a semicircle at one end of the barn. We are at the other end. The little child is set in the middle of us. A tune begins, haunting and quiet, "Oh, Batambong, *ban dohl chhet euy . . ."*

The dancing starts. The little girl twists; her hands stretch and turn, exquisite movements, whispering of ancient temples and a culture winding back beyond record. Shy clapping picks up the beat. Someone turns a bucket over and pounds the rhythm. Someone whispers the interpretation, "Oh, Batambong, beloved province. You are so beautiful. I hate to say good-bye. . . ." Longing for home, such longing.

The dancer in her ragged clothes undulates innocently in the old, ancient way. The soft voices of the singers are haunting. The pigs grunt. The thatch sheds on our hair and garments. The quiet clapping, the muffled rhythm of the bucket, the longing.

All of a sudden the moment comes together; the terrible, unspoken mourning falls back. Hush, be still. *Life rises in Prasat. You can hear it if you are quiet.* "Oh, Batambong, *ban dohl chhet euy . . ."*

This is the mystery of mankind, the most imponderable, unanswerable question. We are eternally resurrecting, starting again, beginning anew. We dance on the mourning places, spin dreams out of the broken shards. It is a wonder, is it not? How do we find the strength to survive? Why does renaissance occur? Where do we draw the waters to wash the ashes from our hair? Why do so few of us lose our minds?

Grief sits in the longhouses. Mourning calls to its companions. But a child dances in the dark shadows. The men sing the old songs. A man marries again; he takes a woman to wife. The bridegroom walks under an umbrella, under the canopy of the village's protection. Rain falls upon a thirsty earth.

Walk gently in Prasat. Life rises. It is a wonder. Stand in awe.

7   Every Man's Child
Calcutta, India, April 13, 1980

Calcutta is a city of refugees. This concrete quarter is blackened by the incessant smoke of pot fires and is unredeemed by the parks and boulevards and elegance of wealthy bureaucracies. It is abraded by the millions who have fled to it seeking sanctuary. Drought drives them from the countryside. Poverty snarls at them, stalks them out of the small villages.

Toward the middle of our journey, we rode through the streets of Calcutta at night, our host an Indian who loves Calcutta, this one place in the world that best gives meaning to the word *teeming*. It swarms with energy, with burdened humanity, with honking, with prolific, abandoned, and importunate life.

After a while I stopped counting the bundles of tossed human rags, dumped upon the nighttime pavement. The sidewalk is home to thousands, gray mounds of indistinguishable color. Here they live. Here they die. Here the young children sell themselves into prostitution so the family can eat the food of this insidious barter. Here young women plunge headlong into old age: haggard, gaunt, severely used.

The merciless 114-degree heat of the next days reminded me of flammable torture. Wispy shadows wilted in the unremittent glare. One skinny spigot provided water for the hundreds who inhabited a city block. Women brought their cooking bowls from the third-floor tenements or from their homeside curbs and washed them on the streets. They yanked their dusty children and doused their heads in these thin fountains. The chalky powder of a concrete foundry blew silt into the gaping cracks of countless old buildings. The din tolled. Here cacophony increased.

I bathed three times a day to wash away the smudged grit and sweat. This ablution distinctly impressed me with privilege.

There is an old saying: So goes India, so goes the world. If true, one look at Calcutta should give the rest of us indisputable pause.

A child was asleep midday on the pavement outside the Grand Hotel. The city has millions of faces, but this one shifted the veil of my fragile curtain again. The feet of a thousand passersby pattered down this boy's dreams. The sleeper's feet were bare; the concrete beneath him worried his naked, unprotected flesh. How old? I guessed he must be about eleven, exactly the age of Joel, one of our sons.

Where was this child's mother?

If I were mother to this boy, wouldn't I wipe the dust from his cheeks, push the hair from his eyes, scold a little, laugh at finding him, draw him into my arms, kiss his face? Wouldn't I insist on something for him to eat and a bath and a clean change of clothes? Wouldn't I tuck him into bed?

I tried to imagine a child sleeping outside the Hyatt Regency on Michigan Avenue in Chicago.

Who was this child's mother? What if I were a mother and could not do these things: could not find the boy or give the ritual back rub or pull the covers under his chin? What if my soul was seared, its center scarred with gnarled nodules of tissue, a wound so vexatious I would not care whether my son slept on the frying-pan pavement of Michigan Avenue while unfeeling pedestrians cast glances on his unguarded nakedness?

We went to visit the Home for the Destitute Dying, that shelter established by Mother Theresa to care for those at the ultimate end of need. She was lecturing in another city and one of her fellow workers, a young man with shining eyes, answered our questions and graciously welcomed our intrusion. Driving across town, we toured the orphanage of the Missionaries of Charity, founded as well by this remarkable woman to care for abandoned children.

Somehow I was not disappointed to have missed meeting Mother Theresa, though I had written about her and followed her work even before she was an international figure. She is amazing, no doubt of that, but not nearly so unusual as people believe.

I suspect the world is filled with Mother Theresas.

They are the young student volunteers who get their feet wet in the streams of world crises. They shovel excrement out of the hallways of grim concrete buildings. They mix the porridges and blood soups that stave off starvation. They loft the dancing bubbles that gladden hearts on resurrection day. They are the doctors who hide themselves in the *barrios* and vine-guarded jungles and the sand-blown deserts of the world. They are the milk mixers and the old missionaries who have spent a lifetime in a culture other than their own, all for love.

These are the ones who believe in nativity. They serve misery with shining eyes. They mend. They do not hesitate to become mother to the child sleeping in the street. In their heart of hearts, like my father, they know these children are their own. Quietly, quietly, they believe.

Often, we look at chaos and conclude, there is no God.

But what do we conclude when we look at good?

What is our response when life insists on tagging after us like a cheeky child whose exuberant joy keeps us from despair and who ignorantly refuses to regard death for long? What do we say when music is heard again in the death camps? What do we say to the deft needles of the fissure menders? What is our cry to those who dare to mother every man's child?

The world is filled with Mother Theresas. We just do not know their names.

Goodness is the only answer to the demon cat that claws at the fabric of our existence.

8   The Awe of Creation
Waterman, Illinois, May 1977

I bought a secondhand beehive one summer. At the time, it seemed a terribly important thing to do. However, busy days prevented me from any more than one quick investigation of the hive, and yet that one look overwhelmed me. I was stunned by a glimpse of the intricate society of these my bees.

One spring, years before my journey, the children and I, novice beekeepers all, set out to discover the wooden hive I had carefully hidden in the undergrowth of the five acres we let grow wild at my father's farm. Our heads were covered by old hats swathed with veiling; our hands were protected by oversized "sting proof" gloves. Our wariness was not in the least diminished by my mother calling gaily from her door, "It's sure been nice knowing you!"

Carefully, we lifted the lid from the hive and watched the enormous activity in this small cage, this lilliputian society, so complicated, so complete. Prying the frames apart with special tongs, we slowly eased one from the topmost super (the box that forms the upper floor of the bee skyscraper). It fell, the bees buzzed angrily, and we watched as the multicylinders dropped their golden juices.

Some of the cells sheltered tiny larvae, which we could vaguely see through the opaque wax. Enthralled, the children and I watched tiny antennae thrust through the walls. Then a fuzzy head emerged, and slowly—slowly—a new-formed brown and yellow body clambered up.

"Oh!" we chorused spontaneously, and carefully eased the infant back into the depths of the hive.

After carrying the frame into the kitchen, we cut out the luscious honeycomb with a carving knife. All of us were reluctant to waste the other half of the frame, to wantonly destroy those brood cells loaded with life in its various stages of bee development.

"Oh, look! Another antenna! And another!"

We returned the half-ravaged frame to the hive. Perhaps, in the environs of the apiary, this devastation is considered a natural disaster.

One tiny insect clambering from its birthing chamber had filled my children and myself with awe. Nativity had hushed us again.

All nativities have meaning, whether it is the advent of a new idea—some concept struggling through the fertile underground of imagination—or whether it is the multiplication of cells viewed beneath the examining lens of the microscope. Each holds the power to evoke faint but recognizable awe from its human witness.

"Oh!" we gasp involuntarily.

All nativities have meaning, and interestingly, it is the natural tendency of the human spirit to exclaim at the moment of birthing. I know of no fathers, though there may be some, now admitted to the once-sancrosanct chambers of the delivery room, who will not swear that they witnessed a miracle when their child was born.

We may become overfamiliar with nativity. I felt this way the summer our pets had a total of eleven puppies. It was a wonderful education for the children. But eleven mongrel puppies?

We may sigh with relief when the birthing process is completed. I have had more articles and books delayed in the birth canal than I care to count. But nativity, the birth itself, is able to evoke a response that most often borders on awe.

Why is it that I sense wonder at birth—whether it occurs in the exercise of a brainstorm session or in the agony of a delivery room or in the delight at spring fields when honeysuckle rises on the bushes and wild asparagus peeps from around the weeds?

Is it because each new birth is a new beginning as well, filled with labor but inherent with promise? And in this world, where our dreams are so easily dashed, don't we need beginnings? Can we exist without promise? To start afresh, to be filled with new hope, to write a poem, to compose music, to stand in awe—these are all the elements of birth. To be united in love, to stand in wonder at the results of union—this is nativity.

And awe, the feeling of wonder, is to me, an intimation of godliness. I think that on an instinctive level, the human spirit knows this. In nativity, whether we recognize God's existence or not, we become partakers of the nature of the Holy One. The initial impulse of creation, regardless of the finished product or of the intent of the human maker, is a godlike emanation. Here we become colaborers with the Creator. For the moment, we enter into mystery.

And a child is the ultimate promise. As poet Rabindranath Tagore has said, "Life's aspirations come in the guise of children."

That is why we stand in awe.

The sun rises. A little boat leaves the coastal waters of a far-off country. A garden is planted. A border is crossed. An architect takes pen in hand. Paint is mixed; the canvas is waiting. Bent twigs for a hut to shelter newly arrived refugees are planted in the ground. A woman weaves a basket. The line moves slowly through immigration. Unto us a child is born.

See, how the world is filled with nativity. . . .

VI   The Departure

1   The Final Birth
Wheaton, Illinois, July 13, 1979

Death stalks the refugee camps. It leaves anguish where it walks—there and in
our own lives. But because of the swath it scythes in the camps, its utter
disregard for age or youth, the unnecessary quality of starvation and man's
inhumanity, it is more tragic there. It hints at an evil that is corporate,
incarnate, and beyond the individual.

Yet death meets us in our world as well. Grief is a common garment.
My father's death helped me to apprehend some of the meaning of death in the
broader world. Though pain is individual, it makes us common. We suffer
alone in order to be able to say, "I understand."

My father's middle name was La Rue, after his mother's maiden
name. The La Rues were descendants of the Protestant Huguenots who fled
the religious repression of Roman Catholic France three hundred years ago.
One of my great-great-great-grandmothers indentured herself to escape this
persecution.

She crossed the Atlantic in a boat migration of this earlier generation,
only to find that the crooked master at her destination intended to sell her
children. She fled with two of them, never to find the third again. I am a
descendant, through my father, of a refugee—my father who is dead.

My dad is a little like the father in Hugh Leonard's play *Da,* that pesky
old Irishman who even after death follows his son around. But then, maybe it
is in the nature of fathers to haunt their children's work.

My father frequently insisted that mother and I would have nothing to
write about were it not for him. Though I hotly denied it at the time, perhaps in
the long run it is true. One of my first published articles was a human interest
piece about daddy's handkerchief, which was run on Father's Day in the
Chicago Daily News. He seems to have crept, unbidden, into many of my
latter works as well. Certainly many of his values dominate the world view
from which I write.

Many of my father's students have written to me since his death. "I
wouldn't have made it through school except for him," is a frequent
comment. Recently, one woman in her early fifties spoke to me personally
after a seminar I had conducted.

"I studied voice with your father," she began, then stopped, caught

98

with the emotion that was beginning to choke her. "Your father was really the only father I ever had."

These comments are gratifying for a daughter to hear, and after his thirty-some years of teaching, they come my way regularly. The one I love the most, because it seems to capture my dad best, is one from a woman who had been on a music team, which it was his responsibility to train.

"I wasn't a music major but a member of a women's trio. As I recall, we were three of the ugliest, most awkward, most self-conscious coeds that ever walked a college campus. Your father was wonderful with us. I remember those two hours that first afternoon. By the time we were done, he had convinced us that not only were we the most beautiful of young women, we were the most talented. . . ."

This is one of the values he impressed upon me: People are beautiful; they are wonderful; they are important.

Mother and I were with my father when he died. It was a long dying actually, starting with the moment he drove home from their retirement farm—mixing his words, putting together odd sentences, which were the first symptoms of the encephalitis. This brain fever was to make the next 4½ years of his life an intricate kind of torture for himself and his family.

Incapacitated, incontinent—these are the words that describe some of the brain damage he sustained. *Aphasia*, a disturbance in language function, is another. They are horrible words when they touch someone you love. We communicated inadequately through gestures and simple sentences and direct commands.

And we brought children's games to the nursing home where he was finally placed. They were all for toddler-level development and encouraged basic manual-visual coordination. A simple, fifteen-piece wooden puzzle was cause for what seemed like excruciating labor. There were small improvements, some that raised fierce hope, but despite our efforts, he slowly, eventually inched downhill.

One afternoon I brought my daughter to the nursing home to visit "Boppa," the nickname given to him by our first child and which all the grandchildren used. This was appropriate because my father and grandfather lavished nicknames on all those they loved.

Boppa was sitting in his wheelchair in the common dining room. The lunch trays had been removed, and an old woman had gone to sleep at the table, her head plopped on its surface.

Dad's clothes were always in disarray. Buttons popped through the wrong holes, bunching the hang of his shirts and pants. Shirttails slipped out at the waistline. We often had to go hunting in the laundry room for an extra stocking or a warm sweater. Consequently, the patterns—plaids and prints and checks—rarely matched. Confused clothing contributed to the general feeling of his debility.

Melissa brought the checkerboard from the top shelf in the closet of his room and set it upon the lunch table next to the sleeping grandmother. My father had always been a champion at the game. My husband, David, and my brother-in-law often teased each other, "How many times did you beat dad at checkers?" The fact that each can remember an approximate amount ("Oh, two or three times, maybe four") attested to his skill.

After a while, and with a great deal of coaching from his granddaughter—part of which was basically reminders for him to stay awake—dad had cornered her last piece. If she moved, he would jump her and win the game.

But it was his move. Deliberately, he pushed his piece in front of hers in such a way that she was forced to double jump his remaining checkers and take the game.

My mouth hung open in surprise. He reacted instantly with mock dismay, pretending to tickle her for beating him, then looked up at me and gave me a broad wink.

This was a man who had no language but gibberish, about whom the neurosurgeons said that his responses were mostly automatic, who often passed hours in an inarticulate rage of frustration, leaving nurses and family in tears. But with my father, love *was* automatic, and this granddaughter, his child, deserved tokens of it.

There were enough moments like these, moments when the overwhelming personality of my father would suddenly emerge from the gaunt-eyed stare, from the barely suppressed anger, that we his family were constantly on the rack, wondering how much of the man—not the patient, not the invalid, not the aphasiac, but the person—was vegetating in the nursing home.

One incident in particular symbolized the torture of these years. In the beginning, daddy was able to walk, unsteadily to be sure, but much of our

100

efforts were directed in exercising him by strolling around the nursing home. One leg always lifted in an exaggerated fashion as though in his eye the ground before him stairstepped away.

Once I struggled for half an hour in my parents' driveway to get him into the car. The cross-purposes of his brain frustrated my attempts, and the simple motion of bending and flexing became an aggravating tyranny of unsteady joints, all going to the wrong direction. Then, for some reason, he resisted me.

I aimed him face first toward the open door and pushed. He clung with amazing strength, his hands splayed against the metal car edges.

We stopped.

I tried another angle, turning him sideways and attempting to ease him into the car. "Lift your leg, dad. Lift your leg. All you have to do is just sit down on the edge of the seat."

He refused to cooperate.

I backed him all the way to the seat, hoping that its ridge against the knee joints would trigger a reflex. The whole time I was scared to death that he would lose his balance and fall.

Finally, something in his brain triggered memory or willingness, and he slipped into the front seat with the smooth ease this ordinary act usually required—as though we had not been wrestling with each other for the last twenty-five minutes.

I buckled his safety belt and whispered exhausted encouragement. "That's great, dad. Now if we could just do it the same way every time, we'd be in terrific shape. I'm taking you back to the nursing home. We love being with you. We will go out again tomorrow."

When the brain is severely damaged, all the equilibriums are disturbed: balance and space distance and thermostat control and the nausea center. A few minutes after our drive began, daddy had vomited over himself and the front seat. Utterly defeated, we arrived at the nursing home where a kindly nurse gently took him from my care, assuring me that his soiled garments would be immediately changed and he would be put to bed for the rest of the afternoon.

I remember driving the twenty-five miles to my own home, and then stretching myself out on the living room rug and weeping uncontrollably. No one can measure the tears shed during those long four years of my father's terminal illness or the weight of the ones unshed.

Near the end of his life dad was not able to eat solid foods; often even liquids choked him. The natural reflex of swallowing became erratic. He slipped more and more away from us, out of consciousness, staring for longer spaces of time. But he had become strangely reconciled to whatever adamant entity it was his to come to terms with. The rages that had often surfaced were gone, and for the last month a gentle serenity invaded him.

Finally the family gathered, and my sister stayed by his bedside singing the old hymns, some from memory, some from the battered hymnbook. She was an alumna of the music department where he had been employed for thirty-three years. Her voice had been trained by one of his own faculty.

I thought of my father's elbows sweeping as he vigorously directed the church choir in the *Elijah*. No meek bobbing of the wrist for him. His baton battled the air; his feet stamped out the rhythm; his free hand whipped the page of the score. Now his choir loft was here, this room, this quiet place. She was the choir, my sister, his child.

He eased into semicoma. We spoke the words to him usually reserved to encourage women in hard labor. "You're doing fine, daddy. It's all right. Just a little while longer. We're right here, daddy. We love you."

Finally, his eyes closed. The staring was shaded by coma. The wonderful nose poked out of the sheath of skin stretched tight by starving. The pink mole at the ridge of his cheekbone evoked memory. "When I was a little girl," my sister recalled, "I asked him where he got that. He told me that a bird had pecked him. I believed him." It wasn't until she was grown that she discovered he had been teasing her.

The night closed around us. My brother and sister left to find some sleep. The room was filled with his breathing: double time, triple. It was a labored pulling. The lungs filled and emptied with effort. Mother and I sat by the bed, held his hand, swabbed the dry lips, eased the going.

I heard the metronome on our grand piano at home timing a practice. *Clock-clock-clock-clock*. One and two and three and four. One and two and three and four and . . . I remembered Saturday mornings and private voice lessons and daddy giving instructions. The half-scale on the piano—up and down: *da-da-da-da-da-da-da-da-da*. Two chord changes, the half-scale again sliding up and down, *da-da-da-da-da-da-da-da-da*. Two more chord changes, these warm-ups for students and great singers alike, the vocalises.

My dad's voice, "Try *oo*." The response: *oo-oo-oo-oo-oo-oo-oo-oo-oo*. The chord changes. The breathing, double time in meter to the metronome.

How like birth was this dying. As if reading my thoughts, mother said, "I will always remember the sermon the minister preached at your great-uncle Millard's funeral. He said that there are three births in life. There is physical birth. There is spiritual birth. And there is death, the birth to a new life. They are all accompanied by travail."

Toward morning, I stretched down on the other bed, which had been wheeled into my father's room. Exhausted as I was, it was nevertheless impossible to sleep while waiting for death. Soon my mother's voice called, "Come, Karen, he's very close."

The breathing had become shallow, light fluttery butterflies on the edge of his lungs. Tranquillity joined hands with serenity. Mother and I sat by his bed and watched death; the soft words were no longer spoken. We were quiet.

One last breath, then another—interrupted—then the outflow, a sigh. The corner of his mouth twisted upward—muscles contracting? Or did the smile die, too, in that awesome yielding—that grand, ornery, laughter-bending, smile. Did that smile go with him, grabbed from this place into the next?

We wondered aloud if his consciousness floated somewhere in our presence. "I suppose dad is hanging around here. . . ." I stifled my unreasonable urge to shout, "Hey you, daddy! It's done. You're finally free!" I think he would have appreciated my grave dancing—but it might have unhinged the nurses who were hiding his body beneath the bed sheet.

It is an awesome moment to watch a father die. I stood in his room as all the living memories came tumbling together in rude disorder. The time was 6:10 A.M., a good time for birthing.

Daddy at the farm with binoculars watching the rosy day coming and the birds whistling greeting. *A good time for this dawn body, this out-of-the-farmer's-loins body*. All his vacations spent hunting good land. Isn't it beautiful he used to say a hundred, thousand ways.

6:10 A.M. A morning going for this lively father.

I still hear his breathing, double time, when I wake up in the morning,

2   A Father's Love
Bangkok, Thailand, April 5, 1980

I met Mark Hovee in a camp in Thailand and interviewed him in the Food for the Hungry headquarters in Bangkok. Mark was in charge of an over-the-border feeding operation. Hundreds of thousands of starving Cambodians had crossed into Thailand in search of sanctuary, but there were still hundreds of thousands of Khmer people starving back in Cambodia who had not fled their native country. Rice was being distributed by the ton at various checkpoints along the frontier.

A truck loaded with foodstuffs would slip over the border, hopefully with the tacit approval of local Thai military authorities, who were understandably sensitive about the possibility of feeding guerillas actively warring against them. Then Mark and his co-workers would "call the people out" to receive food at the distribution point. Word, passed from person to person, would eventually hail the oxcart brigade, which would carry the rice and small quantities of canned meat and vegetables into the interior.

International attention had questioned over-the-border feedings such as these. Accusations had been made that most of the rice was falling into the hands of insurgent guerilla groups who sustained their war efforts from it, and, consequently, extended the agony of Cambodia.

I asked Mark about this during my interview. He felt confident that the rice was going into the mouths and stomachs of the villagers.

"We would know," he explained. "When the people are called out, they would tell us. We are continually being given assurances that the rice is reaching the villages."

At first this seemed like incredible naivete, but after some thought, it began to make sense. Hungry people with starving families can't afford the luxury of partisanship for long. They need food. Sooner or later someone would have indignantly informed Mark if the rice had been misappropriated.

"Are you in danger?" I wondered.

He smiled, then answered, "It's funny that you should ask that. Just last night, all of a sudden, I was scared to death and prayed, *Oh, God, whatever you can do, just get me out of here.*"

The distribution team had already been shot at once; Communist Vietnamese often sent small patrols to disrupt the feedings; there was always the danger that insurgents, the Khmer Serei (Free Cambodians) or the Khmer Rouge (Communist Cambodians backed by China), would rise out of hideaways.

We studied the maps of Thailand and Cambodia, and Mark identified the positions of the refugee camps for me. Then we sorted out the confusing political influences in Cambodia.

The resistance groups in the country conducting guerilla warfare are the Khmer Serei, non-Communist supported, and the Khmer Rouge. The two groups are now negotiating combining their forces to oust the puppet regime, which is backed by the Vietnamese Communists.

Even the name of the country is confusing. Khmer is the ancient name. Cambodia is the modern one, which was dumped by the Vietnamese for the most recent, Kampuchea (which has historical, pre-Western roots). Khmer, Cambodia, Kampuchea are synonymous.

However, what most interested me was the honest vulnerability of the young man who was patiently informing me of all these vagaries. I wanted to know more about how he had become involved in this rather risky adventure.

His background included three years in the armed services with some time in Korea, a B.A. in political science from Seattle University, a year in Washington, D.C., and in Jerusalem, studying political science and philosophy. His father had been a Baptist minister who died when Mark was twelve years of age.

"Within two years after my father's death, I was a rebel agnostic," he said. "In trouble in high school, in trouble with the authorities, giving my mother a lot of pain.

"After the army, I began to realize I needed something outside of myself. This was a totally personal process, this recognition of inadequacy. It started with an inner struggle that took several months of negotiating with God before I finally relinquished everything.

"I was sitting in a crummy tavern in Bellingham, Washington. I had just had a fight with a friend. I looked at the people around me and identified with them. They were all in a bad state, filling gaps by being in a place like that. I leaned back in my chair and said, '*God, I don't even believe in you. But if you're there, I'm willing to give you all I am.*

"All of a sudden I was filled with an incredible joy and peace and real love for everyone in that crummy little bar. Something gave me assurance that it was more than my delusions that had come into me."

We completed the interview, and because Mark had some grasp of the Thai language, he flagged down a taxi and accompanied me back to the hotel, where we made arrangements to meet the rest of our traveling party for lunch. As we were sitting in the lobby waiting for them to arrive, I asked a question that had crossed my mind before. I kept seeing that twelve year old, who two years after his father's death had become "a rebel agnostic."

"Do you have a need for father?"

Typically honest, Mark answered, "Yes."

"How is need like that expressed?" I pressed.

"It isn't. It isn't ever expressed. It's just carried on the inside of me and sometimes forgotten. I pretend like it isn't there, but it is."

I am like Mark Hovee, filled with a need for father, longing for something I can never have again. I am like the countless refugees in the camps who suddenly become the last in the line of generations—unduly soon, before the time. We are lonely for irreplaceable loving fathers.

Kindness given by older men can be extremely touching. Once my great-uncle, the last living patriarch of that great clan of my grandfather's, visited us in our home. He had just been to the nursing home to see my father. At that point, we had no idea whether my dad would live for another year, or for twenty.

This great-uncle has always had sure psychological instincts. Before retirement, he was a bishop in my father's family's church denomination. A great deal of the dinner hour was spent recreating our childhood pasts: how my brother had misbehaved when he was two, the precocious things we all had said, the dates and times of family gatherings. My uncle understands that this is one of the important gifts the older generation gives to the younger.

Then he turned to me and said, "Karen, you must understand that your father is not in the nursing home. That is not Dick. He is not there. You must not go so often. You have four children to take care of. You must not take the children to see him so often, either." He reiterated these sentences several times to make sure I understood.

With those few words, he instinctively fingered my unspoken guilts. Was I giving enough of myself to husband and children and church and father and mother, or was I neglecting them all?

When the last good-byes had been said and my great-uncle had left to fly back to the west coast where he lives, I walked up to my bedroom, closed the door, and began to weep profoundly.

My husband came to see what was wrong and asked, "What has caused this? Your uncle was wonderful to you."

That was the problem. It had been so long since I had known my father's love. I had simply been unhinged by kindness. How warm this patriarch's concern had been, how uniquely understanding of my private pain. What freedom I had found in his few words: freedom to mourn, to give myself space to heal, to not tear my love in pieces so that it was apportioned in meagre doles. His understanding gave me objectivity to face the emotional torture of my dad's illness.

The words of the old hymn began to rise. *Great is Thy faithfulness, O God my Father.* . . . It had meant nothing when I mouthed it as a little child, wiggling in the hard church pew.

There is no shadow of turning with Thee. . . . It had been a slow song when I was a teen whispering to my friends behind the psalter, with my father giving me scowling looks from the choir loft.

Thou changest not, Thy compassions, they fail not. . . . But now that my father was dying these words were comfort. *As Thou hast been Thou forever wilt be.* . . .

My haunting memories of my father will never be silenced. Often we find ourselves surprisingly vulnerable. Like Mark, I must look ultimately beyond this earth to a heavenly parent, who is the only one able to fill this great and terrible haunting.

Perhaps this is one of the reasons the church in the camp of Khao I Dang has grown from some twenty families to over ten thousand people.

Sooner or later, we must find father.

Great Is Thy Faithfulness

Great is Thy faithfulness,
O God my Father,
There is no shadow of turning with Thee;
Thou changest not, Thy compassions, they fail not;
As Thou hast been Thou forever wilt be.

Pardon for sin and a peace that endureth,
Thy own dear presence to cheer and to guide;
Strength for today and bright hope for tomorrow,
Blessings all mine, with ten thousand beside!

3   The Holy Warriors
Quetta, Pakistan, April 18, 1980

Toward the end of our itinerary, we visited Pakistan. The windswept hills of Baluchistan Province are barren of everything except scrub and rock. Their bleached-bone beauty is replica to all the arid wilderness of the Middle East. Dun camels glide ponderously around the hillocks and barrows. Curly haired goats, spotted and speckled, bound over the hummocks, searching for fodder and playing hide-and-seek with the herdsmen. Small orange red flowers bleed here and there upon the soil.

We were headed to visit an encampment of resistance fighters, the *mujahiddin* (holy warriors) of Afghanistan, which was pitched on this side of the border. Our guide was the son of a Pakistani churchman; both he and his father were spearheading relief programs in this region. Thousands cross the frontier every week, costing an estimated six hundred thousand dollars a day to provide food, shelter, medicine, and clothing for the present refugee population. That adds up to roughly fifty cents a day per person.

In the distance, Afghan refugee tents, some erected over mud-daubed foundations, which act as a barrier against the cold, stretched across the land, modern squatters' settlements. Local residents are predictably nervous about sharing scant water supplies and grazing rights. Authorities shift new arrivals from private acreages to government properties. Often three-to-four families must share a tent, and medical aid is spread thin.

A garish truck adorned with improbable gewgaws lumbered down the highway opposite us, swaying recklessly on its axles. It was loaded with refugees. During winter the Afghans must flee over the border through mountain passes in cold and snow. Many freeze to death or suffer from frostbite. Often Russian aircraft fire upon them. Most are ill or suffering, and the trucks, which transport them to the camps, are a Pakistani mercy.

These refugees were fleeing from the Russian occupation, from the razing of entire villages, from the looting and burning, from fields that have been mined, from forests that have been defoliated, and from starvation. (It has been reported that Hazara families were eating a broth made from the salty soil.)

It was not long before we arrived at the tents of the *mujahiddin*, the holy warriors. Their encampment was like no other camp we had seen. The

110

tents were arranged in military precision, all facing in the same direction, each spaced in a straight line and at an exact distance from each other. I wondered at their placement, so obvious and open and so close to the border. This certainly was not the ragtag guerilla band I had pictured hiding in the hills.

Carefully placed stones marked the path to the commander's headquarters, which stood off to one side from the other tents on a little rise of land. The inside of the tent was as neat as the outside. Dark blue wool had been hand stitched to cover the floor and was tucked cleanly beneath the edges of the lodge. The same fabric upholstered bolsters, which lined the two long sides and were placed to face each other. Maps hung on the canvas walls along with the picture of some ayatollah unknown to us.

In the center of the tent sat the commander, behind a camp table on a raised dais. He was bearded, bareheaded, and wore a light blue chalwar kamis with the sleeves of the shirt rolled in working order above his elbows. He nodded as we entered and calmly assessed us with startling blue eyes.

We sat below him cross-legged on the soft navy wool, leaning back against the bolsters. The man was utterly imposing, his presence filled dark space with authority, with command.

A word was spoken and a young man in the corner stood. His head had been shaven and his broad cheekbones evoked the similarity between the highland peoples stretched in a thin line of resistance across Asia: the Montagnards, the Hmongs. He was tribal, of the Hazara. He bent and left through the pinned tent flap, only to return in a few seconds to serve us green tea, hot and sweet.

The translated discussion began. The commander said little, most of the talking being carried on by a second in command. There were no arms in the camp. In a month these men would move to the border, meet their comrades, and receive weapons as they crossed into Afghanistan. Their families were in comparatively safe places. Before the occupation the men were merchants, teachers, civilians.

One of the men in the tent made a point to our interpreter, belabored it. "The Afghan invasion is not just a takeover of one country, but it is part of a plan of a larger scheme." He had defected from the Afghan military, which is cooperating with the estimated one hundred thousand Russian troops now repressing the country. He had heard the conversation of these Russian soldiers.

111

"Next the Russians will advance into Pakistan, then to Iran, then on and on, even to your own country, the United States. It is part of a grand plan to take over the whole world." He stopped, then said one thing more.

The interpreter passed it on. He had said, "Tell your country."

We, the three Americans in the camp, didn't respond. How could we explain that our country had already heard this; it just did not believe it?

The discussion continued, and we heard the vows that are the battle cry of the *mujahiddin*. "We believe that because of the righteousness and the holiness of our cause, that even faced with two Russians—if we only have a knife against their guns, if we only have one against many—we can kill them. We will fight. We will fight to the last man. And even if all our men are killed, our boys will fight, and then our women and children."

For the Muslim, it is an honor to die fighting against the infidels.

The interview was completed. We moved out of the tent and started to climb into our parked van, but Soloman, our interpreter, called to us. The commander had dismounted his dais and had come to the front of the tent.

"Would you like to see how the men (some several hundred) are fed?" our guide called. "The commander would like to show you."

Slightly surprised, we nevertheless took our host up on his offer and walked over to a huge black pot simmering on an open fire. I noticed that the Afghan commander, down from his elevated platform, looked less like a formidable warlord and more like a man among men: a son, a husband, a father. The wind caught the light material of his costume and molded it against his body.

Soloman picked up a discarded wool stocking from the ground (one woven out of coarse goat's hair), slipped it over his hand, and lifted the hot lid from the huge pot. Clouds of steam rose. He stirred the vegetable-and-bean broth inside with a wooden spoon. "This is *dal*," explained our Pakistani friend, looking ever so much like an accomplished and confident gourmet. I was taken a little aback, remembering his sister's words when we had visited his home: "Soloman doesn't even know how to boil water for tea."

"Soloman," I said, using his given name as much as possible, since it is such a wonderful name and so unusual to my own people. "How did you know to do that?" I nodded to the stocking over his hand and the wooden spoon.

He leaned toward me as though to reveal some great culinary secret, then said, "I saw one of the men do this the last time I was here."

We laughed. It was such an ingenuous confession. Suddenly, I was aware that the Afghan commander standing beside me was also laughing. Thinking back, I realized that he had been discreetly laughing through the whole interview in the tent. This was a canny sheik, this warlord in the wilderness. He had not been speaking our English, but he had understood every word of it.

Huge, round, flat breads are baked on the open surface of mud ovens, one side browned, then turned. This is *nan*. It and the *dal* are staple food items. The commander bent, lifted the hot, whole wheat *nan* and broke off a piece, offering some of it to each of us. We sampled the coarse baked meal. The man's eyes were startlingly blue above his outstretched hand.

I gazed on the windblown hills, the great sweep of rolling terrain. The faint old rose of dusk was creeping across the land. Little burros wandered between the tents and down the hills. Afghan warriors gathered brush for the cooking fires, which burnt in regular locations among the orderly tents. The odor of *nan* and *dal* intrigued our nostrils. It was day's end, time to go.

The Afghan leader shook our hands, mine last. The rest were scurrying toward the van. I withdrew my hand, but he did not let go. I said, "Good-bye and thank you so much again," and for an instant longer he still kept my hand. I looked into the blue eyes and tried to decipher an unworded message.

Finally we were all loaded into the van, and we headed back through the Baluchistan countryside to the city of Quetta, through the sunset casting pink and purple shadows on the hills. Someone in the cab spoke, "Was it just me or was that man filled with incredible charisma?"

We all agreed that it had been an unusual encounter, but I privately thought about that handclasp. What had it meant?

I found myself wishing that the commander had not come down from his dais. He should have stayed protected within his imperious charisma, haughty and silent. The leader in the tent with the guarded expression, surrounded by war maps and fighting manuals was somehow in control, even in command, of death.

But the banter of our conversation had warmed him; our joyful enthusiasm had drawn him.

The man who had called us from our van had become utterly human, familiarly lonely for company. He had laughed at our jokes, understood our language, broken off fragments of bread and shared them with us. The blue eyes and the touch of the hand had said: "I need this laughter, this lightheartedness in this sunset afternoon; I need this brief reminder of women far away in a safe place."

For that one moment he had been unguarded, utterly vulnerable, subject to the winds that shifted his garments, to the cold storm blowing over his land.

I remembered the outdated weapons described by the warriors, weapons they employed against the modern military might of the Russian invaders. ("If we had knives, we could fight against their weapons," declared one Afghan. "But we don't even have knives.")

Oh, stay on your dais, I wanted to warn him. *This is warfare. Draw the hauteur of command around you. It is important not to show your vulnerability. Do not be fragile in any way. Death always finds the chink.*

We need men to be husbands, men who know how to be fathers.

4 The Final Warning
Enoolpopong, Kenya, April 21, 1980
Mogadiscio, Somalia, April 29, 1980

The Maasai elders, the *Ilpayiani,* have studied the entrails of a goat. They have seen the future in the bloody configurations. It is determined. The great dog drought will stretch out upon Maasailand. He will roll down upon the pampas of the Great Rift Valley, which incises Africa nearly west to east. He will rub his huge back on the concave floor that slopes up to the mountains: Kilimanjaro, Kenya, Meru, and Lengai.

Then he will trot to the precious watering holes and lap them dry; he will drink and empty the seasonal rivers. His ribbed belly will plop upon the land, suffocating the vegetation. He will pant hot breath over Kenya and Tanzania, the historic grazing territory of the Maasai. Then he will sleep, a slumber not to be disturbed. He will not be wakened.

Old dog drought is sleeping now in the East Horn of Africa.

One relief worker is quoted as saying, "You find the human tragedy so staggering that you retreat into thinking about the problem as would a factory manager, in terms of mere supply and demand: How many people are dying? How many can we reasonably hope to save? How many tons of food are needed? How many tons have been shipped? Where will we get the trucks? Individual stories are lost in the bustle. Death from starvation treats every victim the same."

During the last stop of our journey, we sat in Mogadiscio, the capital of Somalia, with the dignified official who is responsible for the huge burden of Ethiopian refugees now swamping his tiny country. The East Horn of Africa is the crisis center of the world now. It is from here that the cry of prostrated humankind must be heard.

The old sand-hued hotel where we were staying was beached beside a bay of the Indian Ocean. Charmingly, the refugee director's grandchild, Ahmed, suddenly appeared to wish his grandpa good evening, then to be whisked off to his own home by his father. I was hungry for my own children and my attention began to wane. I hadn't quite reached the point of compassion fatigue, but my ability to absorb any more statistics was definitely diminishing.

Emotionally I was turning toward home.

Suddenly, our host's words caught my attention: "The eye is the best teacher."

I thought of the hundreds and hundreds of refugees we had seen. We had walked step after step on the dusty ground of numerous camps both inland and seaside in numerous countries. The sun had blistered us, simmered our body temperatures. We had brushed, touched, talked with, patted, shaken hands, bumped against, bowed to, and been pressed by multitudes.

In the lobby of that hotel, with old marble floors and a once-grand staircase, I understood the apostle John's persuasion: "That which was from the beginning, which we have heard, which we have seen with our eyes, which we have looked upon and touched with our hands . . . we proclaim also to you . . ."

To have brushed against, stood beside, clasped, conversed with, and shared food with a man in whom you found no disappointment (when all your life you had met nothing but disappointment) had been enough to convince this one disciple. For John, the eye was the best teacher. Often, it is enough.

The meaning of the phenomenon of the modern refugee is utterly significant. We must not allow ourselves to lounge comfortably behind our backyard canopies when a simple demographic map of the world will clearly show how fragile that comfort is.

As much as any other phenomenon, the refugee is a metaphor for our times. Melaku Kifle, the refugee secretary of the All African Council of Churches, expresses the powerful significance this massive dilemma communicates to us. "It is the refugee who reveals to us the defective society in which we live. He is a kind of mirror through whose suffering we can see the injustices, the oppression, and the maltreatment of the powerless by the powerful."

The refugees, those who resettle in our country as well as those who remain in the scattered camps of the world, give me an opportunity to link myself to the world community. It is time to discard the kind of arrogant provincialism, which refuses to lend clothes when the next-door neighbor's house burns. For that is how close we really are. We have gone beyond the point where the fall of some unpronounceable nation will have no influence on our own existence. That day has vanished. Our economies are too intertwined, our dependencies too symbiotic.

I have seen the refugees and been moved by the great beauty and the sufferings and the longing of these people. They are common beauties, common sufferings, and common longings. Common to us all. But the refugee experiences them en masse and at terrifyingly accelerated levels. We partake of these things as well, but privately, diminished in that we have no community.

I have looked and seen the refugee within me, within us: that wanderer in each man's and woman's soul, which does not allow hope to be extinguished.

I have seen and become convinced that it is the refugee who can help us—help us by reminding us. The refugee can teach us what is truly of value. He can remove the fragile curtains of our personal illusions.

The curtains of the nations are also being moved, shoved against by these masses. To what extent, no one knows. But perceptibly, they are beginning to sway. What coming finality will tear them asunder?

> When you come down to it there are very few real racists. There are just people whose habits have been disturbed. We are a disturbance. That's the word. Because we show you in a terrible way how fragile the world we live in is. . . . You didn't really know this, in your skin, in your life. You knew it, but in a theoretical way. The massacre of the Jews was your first warning. We are your second warning. I think it is the last. . . .
>
> A Cambodian refugee, exiled in Paris, whose husband was killed by the Khmer Rouge.

6   The Circle of Family

Wheaton, Illinois, Christmas Day, 1980

A full moon shines beyond the window. I can see it beneath the curve of my husband's chin. Exhaustion has wakened me, but I hold myself still to reserve strength. It is early Christmas morning of the year of the refugee journey. By the moonlight in our uncurtained bedroom, I trace the shadow of sleep that has creased his cheek. Quietly, so as not to disturb, I press close to his warm comfort. I should drag myself from the bed. Our child sleeps in a hospital, tubes attached to his arm, and I want to slip into his room before he wakes.

I stay, suspended for a moment in this warming. It touches my aching back and bones and soul. Waking is always a moment of awe. I am learning to never take it for granted. This is the only moment I can hold—this now. This is the only part of time about which I am sure.

One of the children in our smallest son's class died from cancer a week before Christmas. Jeremy was supposed to act, with other friends, as a pallbearer; but he and his brother, Joel, caught the flu. They had recovered quickly, but on Monday morning Joel began running a temperature again.

I smooth the hair on my husband's forehead, push back the lovely gray from his temples. I feel his tiredness. The moon is sinking into the woods beyond the window, and they are a shimmer of shadow and shade and snow.

I sent a Christmas arrangement to the family whose child had died of cancer a week before Christmas, knowing that with months of waiting and watching in a hospital, with the cold realities of a funeral in a frozen world, there would have been no time to think about holidays.

How awful, I thought, *to lose a child at this time of year. Whenever it comes again, it will drag, remembering mourning with it.*

I place my open palm on the curved neck of my sleeping husband, near where the artery flutters. I feel the life, the beating onward. I whisper prayers. He is older than I am. I have seen the statistics that state I have a 70 percent chance of being a widow someday. I know, as surely as I know anything, that I am not exempt from loss. I hold no guarantee on life.

When my son Joel became ill again, I spent all day in his room waiting. He began vomiting. A small rash appeared on his skin. I made an appointment to take him to the family doctor. The vomiting stopped. His fever, which had been around 103, went down to normal; the rash began to fade. False alarm. I canceled the appointment.

But I took him to bed with me that night, for some reason, still watchful. Soon the vomiting began again, and not long after that his mind slipped beyond me. I called David from the living room couch and he phoned his brother, a surgeon, who advised us to take Joel immediately to the emergency room.

"I don't want to play," he cried, vomiting again as we bundled him in a warm blanket. His words were incoherent. He was gone from me.

The night was crisp and dark. The emergency room doctor knew us. Joel had been an unwilling patient of his before. He took one look, had a specialist called, pointed out the little purple rods, which now stood on our child's flesh, and gave a preliminary diagnosis: "Meningitis." Then to prepare us, he said the doctor words, straight forward and unelaborated, "This is a very sick child."

Meningitis, inflamation of the lining of the spinal cord and the brain. I said the word in my mind carefully, not too loudly.

"Mom! Mom! Get off of me," my child cried as the nurses curled his back and held his legs for the spinal tap. His eyes were not focusing. I was holding my heart a half a room away.

David's mother had a brother and sister who died of meningitis. My mother's best friend had died in her teens of—My friend's mother, a missionary in China, while fleeing from the Communists had—And now—

I was aware that if my son lived, one of the options would be brain damage. Why had I taken out the medical encyclopedia on Monday morning after I had kept Joel home from school and looked up meningitis?

Brain damage.

We had been here before. I knew it intimately. I watched for 4 ½ years as it took my father. I wanted to hold it off, put the heel of my palm against its forward motion and stiff-arm it away from us.

But we are not exempt. I hold no guarantee on life. My father is dead. Men and women and children are dying all around the world. A little friend of Jeremy's died of cancer. There were wispy threads of snow on his funeral day. My great-grandmother planted six of her offspring in the ground while they were yet children. My grandmother died in childbearing.

We are not exempt.

Death stalks us.

My child was wheeled to an isolation room. Antibiotics were fed into his arm intravenously. My brother-in-law came to the emergency ward, my husband's father and mother; my sister-in-law met us in the hallway. My brother arrived a little later, his Bible in hand. David called my sister in Florida and had her notify my mother, who lives there in the winter.

Here we were gathered, watching over this child who might be slipping into the waters. Here we were meeting as we should always meet, but rarely find the time or desire. Death always calls us together.

Why ever death? Why not life?

I had been here before, watching incoherence and slipping and coma. I had stood by my father's bed on Easter Sunday as he lay in a coma before recovering enough to lead years of brain-damaged existence. Yet a reality, warm and comforting, had flooded me then, giving me quiet, easing the heartache.

This assurance was here now, in this child's room.

I knew—again an instinctive knowledge—as soon as the antibiotic began flowing into my child's blood, and he opened his eyes and recognized me—that he was safe.

Lying in my husband's arms on this Christmas morning before light dawns, I roll into his sleeping form, touch toe to toe, knee to knee, midriffs and foreheads. *This is privilege,* I think. The circle of my family has not been broken. From the utter depths of my soul I know I have no special promise of living; no child is beyond death's jurisdiction, no husband.

Help me, I plead. *Help me to cherish, to hold, to enjoy, to honor the gifts.* I have learned I can only hold this present moment. I must love it with all of my being.

Tears have not come through this crisis. Now I begin to quietly weep. I pull the soft flannel of the old nightshirt, which my gram made for my husband, against my face. I breathe its familiarity, wipe my tears on its well-washed softness. I must get up soon to prepare my living son for nativity morning. I want him to wake and see me by his bed. I want him to be reassured by familiarity.

Lying there I remember the words of T. S. Eliot:

The great snake lies ever half awake, at the bottom
   of the pit of the world, curled

In folds of himself until he awakens in hunger and moving
   his head to right and to left prepares for his hour
   to devour.
But the Mystery of Iniquity is a pit too deep for mortal
   eyes to plumb. Come . . .
Be not too curious of Good and Evil;
Seek not to count the future waves of Time;
But be ye satisfied that you have light
Enough to take your step and find your foothold.

I bend my head up and carefully kiss my husband's chin: the closed eyes, the sleep crease. For the present, we are safe.

There are some things worth pressing for, worth holding onto, worth fighting for. This. This circle of family. This now I will grasp in utter gratitude. This man. This one I will cherish.

I vow in the sleeping strength of his arms to ask for no more: to refuse to expect endless days ahead or health or wealth or old age. All I want is the rare strength to cherish what I have—this man, these children, this life. To lift my heart and celebrate the incredible beauty of a man and woman who love. To breathe unending thanks for enough food for *this* meal and enough courage for *this* terror. And to pause enough to recognize the glory in each hour.

I wipe my tears again and slip from the warm love into the cold bedroom to prepare to go into the frozen Christmas morning. I am awed that a new day is rising again; I watch the faint line of pink break over the woods.

Dressed, I pause by the bedside and whisper, "Merry Christmas." I look out the other window, in the opposite direction, and notice that the moon still bathes the mass of winter trees in dim light. It is both day and night.

My husband rouses, pulls me down to him, and wonders, "How are you doing?"

How am I doing? I am exhausted, weepy, still a little shaken, slightly unstrung. But I'm dancing in celebration all over this nativity morning. Joy comes, fiddling a backwoods country rhythm. It is praise.

Life is rising.

"I am fine," I respond. "A little tired, but fine. Bring the children when everyone is awake. We'll open stockings all together in Joel's hospital room.

"Merry Christmas," I whisper again. I have spoken these words every year, all my life. Happy gift day. Joyful nativity. Have I been speaking incantation? Is this what ultimately pushes back the haunts of graveside and hard ground and hearse? New birth. The birth of the Child Savior.

Merry Christmas. These words have never before, in all my life, sounded like a benediction. But they are.

It is true. My fragile curtain has been torn. The world is not well. I am not safe. I know that I, and the ones I love, are only a breath, an exhalation away from not being. The bittersweet beauty of knowing this makes living rare.

It is one of the secrets of being a refugee.

Appendix

There are many worthwhile relief and development agencies in the world. Listed below are just a few of the many with competence and merit:

1. **Action Internationale Contre la Faim,** 13 Rue d'Uzes 75002 Paris, France.
2. **American National Red Cross,** 17th and D streets NW, Washington, DC 20006.
3. **CARE, Inc.,** 660 First Ave., New York, NY 10016.
4. **Catholic Relief Services,** 1011 First Ave., New York, NY 10022.
5. **Christian Aid Division of the British Council of Churches,** P.O. Box No. 1, London SW9 8BH, Great Britain.
6. **Food for the Hungry International,** 7729 East Greenway Road, Scottsdale, AZ 85260.
7. **International Council of Voluntary Agencies,** 17 Ave. de la Paix, 1202 Geneva, Switzerland.
8. **International Rescue Committee, Inc.,** 386 Park Ave. South, New York, NY 10016.
9. **Lutheran World Relief and Lutheran Immigration and Refugee Service,** 360 Park Ave. South, New York, NY 10010.
10. **Oxfam,** 274 Banbury Rd., Oxford OX2 70Z, Great Britain.
11. **Save the Children Fund,** Jebb House, 157 Clapham Road, London SW9 OPT, Great Britain.
12. **United States Committee for Refugees, Inc.,** 20 West 40th St., New York, NY 10018.
13. **The US International Development Cooperation Agency,** Washington, DC 20523.
14. **World Relief,** 450 East Gunderson Drive, Carol Stream, IL 60187.
15. **World Vision International,** 1415 Cahuenga Blvd., Hollywood, CA 91016.
16. **Youth with a Mission,** 9918 Commerce Ave., Tujunga, CA 91042.